THE LEFT COAST
OF PARADISE

California and the American Heart

JUDITH MOORE

Most of the text of this book first appeared, in different form, in The San Diego *Reader* and The East Bay *Express*.

Published in the United States of America by
Soho Press, Inc.
One Union Square
New York, NY 10003

Library of Congress Cataloging-in-Publication Data

Moore, Judith, 1940-
The left coast of paradise.

1. California—Social life and customs—20th century.
2. California—Popular culture—History—20th century. I. Title.
F866 . 2 . M635   1987   979.4'053   87-20481
ISBN 0–939149–03–6

Manufactured in the United States of America
FIRST EDITION

For

John Raeside

Contents

THE LEFT COAST OF PARADISE

POPCORN AND TAR

1

POPCORN AND TAR

Ask newcomers to California, "Why here? Why not Texas, or New York, or Iowa?" and they will tell you about where they used to live, or someone they knew back there. But they don't tell you why.

My grandmother was the *why* for me. In the twenties she fled Indianapolis and her husband, dropped my mother off in Oklahoma, and zigzagged to Los Angeles, where she opened a popcorn stand near the La Brea tar pits. Family legend puts her in L.A. with a man, someone from Indiana. The man. Where did the man go?

By the late thirties my mama had married. My grandmother—Grammy—was back in the Midwest and alone, her hair gone pure white. In 1951, blue eyes larger each day as she rode out her final illness, she would turn to my mother, grip her hand, and say, "When I get better. . . . When I get better, we'll go to Californey."

My mother would say, "Yes, Mama. Yes." But even I knew it was a plea for more life, not wanderlust, and that she would not make it back.

California took seed in my mind not as Hollywood, or orange groves and ocean beaches, or freeway hell, but as paradise, where even after you wore hope down to the bone, hope didn't die.

Growing up I pushed back extravagant tendencies that I identified with my grandmother. I wanted my life clean, scored by the juvenile Mozart—a few woodwinds would do—and not the symphonic bombast that followed Grammy. I held tight to the ropes that bounded decency. I stayed in the lines. Then I slipped. Near forty, I took up sins of the spirit. I ran off to California to find more.

Berkeley in the postradical eighties is what I found. Smoke of mesquite barbecues had replaced tear gas. Menus were the new manifestoes. And dining took as much time as demonstrations. The circle skirts and brocade sheath dresses, and strapless tulle gowns I wore in high school, hung in boutiques as vintage clothing. Bob Dylan was as wrinkled as Abe Lincoln, and "Blowin' in the Wind" and "Abraham, Martin, and John" played in elevators. It didn't matter. A woman of "a certain age" and proud, newly poor, and without job skills, I trusted California to take me in. Virtually seasonless and always forthcoming with new permutations of human personality, it was not likely to punish me. In the temperate-zone, main-street town from which I had run, the township defined character and determined fate. In California you played out your life by ear. You improvised.

You could be what you said you were. Beginnings were everywhere; you didn't need a past. At worst—and I feared the worst—a Californian could sleep on the beach.

•   •   •

I rented a room with two windows to the west and one to the south. I bought a cheap radio and tried all the stations. I hung bamboo shades and unpacked my few belongings. For the first time in my life I was by myself. I liked it.

Someone opened my door, looked in, and said, "This is a Bedouin's existence." It is.

Hotplate. Cup-a-Soup. Change of clothes. Books. But it has the virtue of being a life I can walk across without every square inch evoking memories. Up early, I catch Aleta Carpenter's gospel music call-in show on station KDIA, "The Boss of the Bay." Why I am riveted by this goes beyond the rendition of "I've Been in the Storm too Long" sung by The Mighty Clouds of Joy. This show is the only place I can hear black folks talk to one another as they do when white folks are not listening. Beginning at 5 A.M., hospital orderlies, janitors, old folks, bus drivers call Aleta and dedicate songs: to "somebody in deep trouble with the law," "to Mrs. Washington, who put her husband to rest this week . . ."

The local paper reflects the environs in its ads—everything from colonic irrigation centers to a vibrator museum. High on nitrous oxide at the dentist's office, I watch him approach and I hear him say, "Just close your eyes and think of Donald Duck." And I do.

I greet the new California day with all the enthusiasm of a beach bunny hitting a great wave. It is gorgeous here, looking out over the bay toward San Francisco. The air slithers down over your skin like a skimpy silk slip. Little wonder the East Bay regularly appears at the top of the *Places Rated Almanac,* its "paradise climate" lauded. Elsewhere virgins were sacrificed, marathon rain dances staged, arrows zinged into clouds. In the American Southwest the Choctaw would hang a fish around a warrior's neck and stand him shoulder-deep in a nearby stream until the rains came. Not here.

A clutch of long-haired vagrants walk past my window with rolls and packs lashed to their backs. A young-faced man, haloed by wild yellow curls, skirts around them to the front of the group. He faces his companions and walks backward. (In seven years I will see countless such elated vagabonds advance on their Pacific goal.) The youth plays a wooden flute. Their packs and blanket rolls bobbing above their heads, the three join hands to form a circle and twirl slowly in celebration. Me, I had taken suitcases, a few books, and walked away from twenty years.

Even if something inside sent you off, what it was still gnaws. You leave for a reason. So there is always something or someone back there niggling. You can't go home again. But you want to . . . if only to cool beer in the creek. I'd take a six-pack. I'd stretch out. I'd play Kenny Loggins. I'd walk under the Douglas fir and cottonwood and alder. I'd walk under the shadows that dapple the carpeting, and sink into the moldering evergreen needles, the damp leaves and dry lichens.

One hundred and five miles into central Washington, over the Cascades range and down onto the eastern foothills into Kittitas County. The highway begins to follow the Yakima River downhill between West Manashtash Ridge and Horse Heaven Hills. The green valley lies twenty-five miles long and ten miles wide. There is the Kiwanis sign, THE EPISCOPAL CHURCH WELCOMES YOU sign, the Pautzke Bait Company's billboard. The town water tower is thick with painted numbers of high-school classes. Downtown is four blocks: shops, the clock tower, the old city hall, the doctor's office where I learned I had a lump in my breast, the clinic where it was removed. "Looks like a piece of chicken fat," I had said.

You may still detest the local politics. You may hate the people or a person, or the climate. You may hate snow. You will have forgotten a lot. But you don't get over the ground. Like the cordillera of hills forming the valley's south and west walls. There, coming down over a shallow riffle, the cold water makes a hard right turn and runs against a basalt cliff, forming a narrow, deep slot. The water fans out into a broad flat, twenty feet wide and a hundred feet long. During a late afternoon, mayflies hatch, and fifty cutthroat trout methodically nip the insects out of the surface film.

I had held the trout's slippery throat tightly, then knocked its head on a rock jutting out over the noisy creek. I rapped the head repeatedly on the shiny hump of granite, as in the last frenzied moments of sex, water splashing the glinting rocks.

I round the corner toward a moment. Three cottonwood trees droop after the long day's heat, leaning over at the turnoff for the county road. I do not turn that corner. The rutted track leads to a riverbank beach, my husband's favorite takeout for rafts. I had portaged the children across there, summer after summer, to sit, sunsuits stripped off, in shallow water. I had splashed them carefully to cool them off and listened to them shriek delightedly, "Oooh, Mama!" The road led also to where I had unrolled my great-grandmother's patch quilt and angrily, almost defiantly, been "adulterous."

I had paddled the river in my canoe through July hot spells. My paddles slapped the green water smartly and skittered the flies. I had tossed cans of water on campfires on both banks, had carried brush for those fires. I had overturned a kayak and struggled, caught in the cottonwood roots that grew along the side of the bank. The force of the river and the tangled roots held me. I had nearly drowned. My husband, downriver from me, yelled, "Don't lose the goddamn paddle!"

It is a small town this noisy river runs through. Perhaps your town is large. Size doesn't matter. One spot always waits, where memory will drag at you.

Each memory comes in an unbroken chunk. I am in the centrifuge of my memory, but the *I* of my memory is no longer the *me* flowing past.

BODY LANGUAGE

2

BODY
LANGUAGE

I was looking for an icon of American summer, the California Aryan teenage madonna. Even though these girls wouldn't be there yet, I got to Pacific Beach shortly before 7 A.M.

A gray belly of fog pressed down on the water, and surf was up and rising, reeking of the amniotic broth that fomented out in deeper waters. Joggers, sweat flying, ran along the white rush of incoming tide. Out of the curving waves rose surfers who wore eerie black wetsuits or kneebuster trunks in neon colors swirled into eye-popping patterns. I tasted salt on my lips.

From nine until ten, after this first shift passed through, the beach stood desolate. Barefoot, I walked south along the mile of cold sand, twenty minutes from downtown San Diego, and then walked back. Walking on the white tide line, I warned myself against starting up some subtextual harangue as to how Southern California is just the Midwest with a beach (which it is), and that these girls were no more and no less than midwestern farmers' grand and great-granddaughters (which they are), heiresses of men and women who came south to gratefully embrace the paradisiacal life of no snow, no cows to milk, and a bit easier money to be had working at the local plant.

Perfect strangers said "Hi!" Locals with oiled dark skin unfolded faded chairs and opened paperback books, the pages swollen and pulpy from days in the salt air. Pallid vacationing families marched single file down through soft sand, each of their faces a replica of the others. Mothers and fathers settled primly on rented chairs. Children took places on white towels carried from motels whose windows looked out over the Pacific. The sun danced on the sea and sparkled off the pastel houses that fronted the beach. The glare flattened the landscape. A zoo of melodies from cassette players and radios ended the solitude.

The early birds got up from their towels. Wearing only their bathing suits, they mounted the steps to the boardwalk. Next to the curb, pickups and vans were parked fender to fender. Windshields glinted. Car radios blasted. Teenage girls in bikinis whirred by on rollerskates. The girls' naked haunches bulged with the minutest exertions of legs or feet. Men's eyes followed. Several girls returned the gazes, even smiled. Others recoiled.

In a shop directly above the beach, racks overflowed with postcards and T-shirts saying LIFE'S A BEACH. Girls began showing up, yawning and perilously naked, hardly covered by the minuscule scraps of bright color.

Their perfection surprised me—their flawless, smooth, browned bodies. The skin was brand new and stretched tight as a drum from pelvic bone down to the juncture of hip and trunk. The girls led with the pelvis, rounded tummies adorable, and stood, a hand smartly on a bare waist, one hip jutted out, as they surveyed the strand of beach.

Cut high on the thigh, pubic hair shaved or chemically dissolved, the girls appear preternaturally long-legged, in the manner of cranes, and as sexless as naked baby dolls. I noted their unearthly beauty and thought they shouldn't have belly buttons.

An apartheid by age was being observed. Only tourists unaware of this informal zoning, and a Cambodian family, heedlessly settled anywhere. The family gathered aluminum pop cans in plastic garbage bags, then settled on the boardwalk to crush the cans with hammers. Even the Cambodian grandmother eyed the girls.

Some were casual: a striped bath towel, Sunblock 15, ChapStick, a bottle of baby oil. They spread towels and stretched out. Others homesteaded. They set out chairs, inflatable pads, AM/FM radio-cassette players, cosmetics cases stuffed with lotions, eye shadow, blusher, and spray bottles filled with water with which to mist themselves. They rubbed scented oil into arms and legs and breasts, adjusted visored sunshades, tucked straps into bikini tops, tuned radios, hummed, pouted.

Sacha drew my interest. She lay on her belly, facing the ocean, brown eyes peering out from under honey-blonde bangs. Her toes wriggled. She was impish and cute, her eyes fixed on two gangly boys tossing a football. Her friend, Marie, crowned with the palest of pale blonde wavy hair, sat crosslegged, facing the boardwalk, her back to the ocean.

"A few girls will come to the beach alone," said Sacha, indicting Marie with a sharp glance. "If they have a car or a brother or boyfriend to drive them. I never come alone."

They came to get a good tan, they said, and to meet cute guys—in that order. What made a good tan? Sacha said, "No lines on your back from your bathing-suit top . . . and really dark." And what made for a cute guy? "Tan, six feet tall, sun-bleached blond hair, blue eyes, white teeth, muscles that aren't too big, and he is really sweet—very friendly."

Sacha said, "There are a lot of cute guys here today," and volunteered that she had never been in love. "I'm too young. At my age you like to flirt, and not be with just one person."

Swarthy boys, striped across their noses and under their eyes with green and yellow zinc oxides to protect against sunburn, waded out of the waves looking like painted braves from cowboy-and-Indian movies. We watched one thin, goosebumped boy emerge from the meringue of surf, his nipples taut with cold. He intercepted a richly tanned blonde whose aqua bikini bottom rode high on her buttocks.

"Who are you down here with?" he asked.

"Nobody," she answered, sucking in her lower lip and drawing her blonde fringe farther over her forehead.

By *nobody,* Sacha explained, she meant she was not with a guy. She had come with two girls and her towel. Sacha pointed out the towel printed with white geese on a field of pale blue terrycloth. The girl and the boy looked toward one another. Neither spoke. Then the boy, yanking at the floral legs of his trunks, turned his eyes toward the group from whose circle he had walked away. He said, "I'm just gonna have some fun."

"See ya," she said, and they parted.

Sacha and Marie did not know them, but guessed they were fifteen. They both liked the white raindrop print on her bathing suit.

Sacha had on a rose-colored two-piece. She has two others. Marie had on a black two-piece with white polka dots. She has five suits. A nearby store with an inventory of six thousand is their favorite place to shop for new ones. They both prefered printed suits and a two-piece to a one-piece. Bathing suits cost twenty-five to thirty-five dollars on sale, and up to forty-five when regularly priced. Most girls, said Sacha, would wear a one-piece only if they thought they were fat, or if they had an ugly stomach, or their parents wouldn't permit them to wear two-piece suits. "And there *are* parents who won't."

Marie concurred: "There's no way of getting by it

because parents like that will check their daughter's tan lines."

The only perceptible breaks in their otherwise unmarred skins are pierced ears. Both Marie and Sacha have one hole in each earlobe. They know girls who have three, four, even five piercings. Sacha wears only the Mickey Mouse ring that she bought at Disneyland. Marie, like many girls on the beach, wears several rings on both hands. "One is Mom's high-school ring," she said, lifting her hand and showing the blue stone.

"Everyone," Sacha said, "wears their mom's high-school ring."

None of the girls seemed to swim. Sacha explained: "When we get hot, we go into the water. We dive in the waves. A lot of girls, though, are afraid to get their makeup streaked."

Both Marie and Sacha are *prokies*—lifelong parochial-school students. Both will be juniors next term at a Catholic high school. Marie said, "People think you go around carrying your Bible and worshiping God a lot. But it's like a normal high school. We cuss. We smoke. We party."

Most mornings Sacha watches soaps in the family room and eats. Usually she puts some frozen french fries in the microwave oven and then puts them on a plate and floods them with ketchup and nacho cheese.

Marie declares, "I am *not* a morning person." Besides watching television, she sometimes reads. This summer she has read eleven of the thirty teenage romance novels available in the Sweet Valley High series. "Lately I've been eating ice cream and cake for breakfast because it was my brother's birthday not long ago."

This is unusual for her. Marie, at five feet, eight, weighs 130 pounds, but she wants to weigh 115. So she drinks instant breakfast mixes two times a day and tries not to eat anything else. "If my mother forces me to eat dinner, I will. But if she doesn't know I haven't eaten dinner, I won't eat all day."

Marie knows an anorectic. The struggle to stay thin "got to this girl's mind. Even though the girl was super thin, she imagined herself as really fat. She would go out with her friends and she would drink Diet Coke. Her friends would eat a burrito and fries. This girl wasn't trying to lie. She would think that she had really eaten what her friends ate. She wound up in the hospital. She could eat only three grains of rice."

Sacha yawned. "I tried dieting for a day, but it only lasted two hours."

• • •

A "cat" is a whip fashioned from nine knotted leather cords attached to a handle—a cat o' nine tails. The cords leave marks like a cat, too. A good one can run thirty or forty dollars. Peggy made hers.

Peggy's leather-lined handcuffs, ankle restraints, riding crops, hood—"actually a half mask," she says—were all bought at a leather shop in San Francisco. Also chains, weights for nipple clamps, eye-bolts, candles for "wax play," and her costumes, which include corsets, garter belts, and the like. She also finds things in hardware stores, tackle shops, and secondhand stores and finds items at yard sales and flea markets.

Five ten, big boned, slender—she is attractive. Her blonde hair, blunt cut, frames her green eyes and falls past her shoulders. She has on a pastel plaid shirt, ruffled at the neck, and a pearl-gray corduroy skirt.

"When I go out I don't dress this way," she says. "When I go out I wear leathers. Leather pants, leather jacket, leather singlet."

Peggy is a feminist lesbian who is into S&M. While she "tops and bottoms" both—is both *S* and *M*—in most encounters she bottoms. She asks for spankings, nipple clamps on her breasts, handcuffs, a blindfold.

"Having your eyes covered increases the suspense. You don't have to see the mundane things. When I top, I like to blindfold the bottom. It's easier for me to top someone who's blindfolded. I'm clumsy, but a really exquisite top makes it look smooth and easy. A good top is hard to find.

"If I had one word to describe what I like as top or bottom it is vulnerability. As bottom, I enjoy my own. As top, I enjoy hers. When I'm bottom I feel openness and trust. I like being tied and forced to submit to what I said I want. When I top, I like discovery—taking a woman a little bit further. I direct her. It's very powerful. In S&M I get to know a woman better in ten hours than in ten months under other circumstances."

Peggy says it is ritual play. As a child it excited her being the Indian maiden tied up by soldiers. It was full of fear and desire, terror and longing. It was real and not.

What S&M is like, she suggests, "is when you shoot somebody and they don't die."

As long as she can remember, images of force and coercion excited her. In sexual fantasies she liked being pushed, humiliated, restrained. "I didn't have rape fantasies so much as seduction. Virgin maiden turned into lusting whore, that sort of thing."

She had been out as a dyke for five years when she first met people into S&M. They were gay men from whom she learned the terminology and "little things." Like "how to identify what a person does by what color handkerchief they wear." She responded immediately and began to wear harness-and-leather on the streets. It was more horrendous, she says, than coming out as a dyke. Lesbian separatist groups trash them, women's bookstores would not stock their literature or let them use bulletin boards to announce meetings. The feminists, feminist-separatists, lesbians, and lesbian separatists see them as "antiwoman."

To add to their problem, many black, working-class, and Jewish women see S&M's play with power inequities and the brandishing of Nazi insignia as insensitive and insulting to the pain and struggle of people raped, oppressed, and murdered by "masters." Although practitioners emphasize consent as part of the ritual "exchange of power," there are objections that such consent is impossible, that their permission does not constitute informed consent. Peggy rejects the general community's definition of politically or otherwise correct sex. She also rejects the argument that, biologically, women have a gentler, more caring nature. I pose a series of questions.

"Do you leave whip marks on your partners?"

"Yes."

"Are you marked by them?"

"Yes, occasionally I am."

"Have you ever drawn blood hitting someone?"

"Yes."

"Being hit?"

"Yes."

"Hot wax?"

"Never. Never use colored candles or beeswax. They melt at too high a temperature."

The pleasure in waxing, says Peggy, is in the suspense, not pain.

Her background? She is a film buff, a registered Democrat, a supporter of the women's music scene. Her family is WASP. Her father is in real estate, selling houses and vacation homes to upper-echelon types. They live in Connecticut. An older sister, married, already has a child, a younger brother is graduating from high school this spring. People outside have an incredibly misguided idea of those who are in it, she says.

"It's not many women's entire life. I have a job. I go to movies. Read. Write letters. I swim three mornings a week. S&M is a framework where my fantasies become three dimensional."

"My mother comes to visit," she says, elaborating on her normalcy. What was her mother's reaction to the "play room" with its obstetrics examining table, rack, stereo rig, black lights? The rack, she says, made her mother uneasy.

"You have to realize," says Peggy, "we use all sorts of everyday items." A big wooden spoon, a paddle, vinyl-coated clothespins in bright colors. There are, of course, high-tech types as well with dungeons and stocks. She is not one of them.

"I do have these shopping sprees though. They come on when I'm interested in someone new."

Her dog collar collection she describes as tacky: "Like pink leather with rhinestones." But each collar has sentimental value. Each was a gift commemorating a moment.

"Non-S&M people imagine S&M as uncontrolled bashing—that a top is a vicious torturer. In fact a good top has incredible sensitivity. She reads you. She often knows before you do what you want. Most people don't realize how much talking goes into a scene, both before and after. You never go into a scene without planning it. And either top or bottom can call off a scene. A 'safe word' is agreed upon beforehand, and if a scene gets too heavy, physically or emotionally, or if it is boring or just not working, *that's* it."

Janet Bellwether's essay, "Love Means Never Having to Say Oops. A Lesbian's Guide to S&M Safety," suggests keeping an extra set of keys for handcuffs and cell doors, admonishes against suspending anyone by wrists or ankles and leaving bottoms tied up and alone for any length of time.

Safety consciousness is promoted. There are workshops in which neophytes are literally taught the ropes—knots. They are also taught hygienic practices necessary for safe piercing of nipples and labia (a practice that Peggy doesn't engage in), for shaving (electric razors work best), and the proper use of whips. Tops practice using a whip accurately and delicately by thwacking pillows. Tops who do not play safely, who drink too much or drug out, and partake with abandon, become known in the S&M circles. People are warned.

"You do not want to get a bad reputation," Peggy says.

• • •

But you live off women, don't you? You take their money?

"Look," he said, exasperated, "what does a wife tell a husband to get him to share his money with her? Nothin' in particular. It's, 'We're in together on this, and I got to bring in mine and you got to bring in yours.'

"If you spend time trippin' a woman why she ought to give you her money, then she's not a ho, and you're not pimpin'."

Gold watch—flat. Pinky ring. Manicured nails. Buffed, not polished. Right under six feet tall, beginnings of a paunch. Starting to bald. High cheekbones. Big brown eyes, irises flecked yellow. Cream-colored Fila velour jogging suit, white Fila cap, doeskin slip-ons. No socks. Maybe 30.

He wasn't going to tell me his name. That wasn't part of our deal. Nor would he tell me where he lived, where his girls lived, what he drove, if he carried a gun, if they carried guns, or how much he—or, they—earned. I asked if he paid taxes, and he laughed hard enough that people looked up from their dinners.

He drew on his mentholated More, looked steadily across the table at me, exhaled smoke. "So, let's do it."

I asked about the word *ho.*

"Where I come from in Mississippi, in Big Foot country—"

" 'Big Foot country'?"

"Yeah, Big Foot country. That's where you only have shoes in the winter. 'Cause you poor. An' your feet spread out, grow big in the summertime. In Big Foot country when the dog's scratchin' at the screen to git in, folks say, 'Open the *do.*' When they ain't had enough gravy ladled onto their potatoes, they say, 'Please pass me some *mo,*' and when they talkin' 'bout a prostitute, they say *ho.*"

There are a lot of myths about it, he says.

"One of 'em is how your pimp dresses. All that tailor-made jewelry: those rings, two on each hand, one of 'em a pinky—his highlight ring—like he gotta bunch of Super Bowl rings on his goddamn hands. Gold necklace made up in his name or his nickname or name of his car. Show-business clothes. Hair permed, rolled up. Conspicuous consumption. The better you can pimp, the less you talk about it. You can tell right off if a guy is jus' down and pimpin'. Or if all he's got in it is clothes and some Mercedes-Benz that ain't never gonna get paid for. I know a pimp, he's got more money 'n most bankers. He drives a Toyota station wagon. His money goes into little businesses.

"There's no doubt that where there's easy money, there's gonna be flash. But how much there is, that's exaggerated."

Did people—neighbors—wonder what he did for a living?

"They may wonder. They assume and they don't ask. With black people, well, jes' write, 'Black people have their own economies. Folks don't make a lot of inquiries.' For one thing, they don't really want to know."

Pimps and prostitutes, are they drug addicts?

"Where there's easy money, there's drugs." He, himself, doesn't do hard drugs. He doesn't work women who regularly use drugs. "A woman has a lot to think about when she's out there. If she's strung out, she's not dependable. She don't keep herself up. She messes up, goes off crazy on you, boosts stuff, brings herself under the eyes of police."

Another myth is that it's a "sex thing" with prostitutes, that they are "nymphos" and attracted to the work for the sex. "Ho's they like to brag on how 'All I had to do was take off one leg of my pantyhose.' Whatever they can do and get away with it, they're gonna do it and git go. Ho's are gonna do the least amount of what they can do to get their money. A lot of tricks just get left right there, sittin' on the bed, holdin' themselves. Tricks don't operate in an area where they can demand a lot of quality control. Who they gonna call, the *Consumer Reports?* The Better Business Bureau? Say, 'Hey, man, Mr. Brown's ho's, they ain't really givin' you no sex. They're just jackin' you off. Fondlin' you an' playin' with you and talkin' jive to you. Then they tell you your time is up.' "

Myth three, he says, is that the pimp has unusual sexual prowess: "You have to sexually please your ho's, that's one of the biggest myths that's gone down. You don't have no time to do no free fuckin'. An' you don't care that much physically

—21—

how she looks or how she is. You learn over the years what tricks accept. You're not havin' this woman for what you like, you're havin' her for what tricks like.

"You hear some pimps talk about, 'Well, I want to make sure she know how to do it.' I say, 'You ain't gonna be the one that's buyin' it. What the hell do you care?' When you hear a pimp braggin' about his sexual powers, don' believe him."

A pimp keeps his "hold" on a prostitute by beating her up.

"There's just no doubtin', there's ho's who have a thing—they like to be abused. You find that in some housewife psychology, the ones who see an ass-whippin' as a form of attention. After the man beats her up, he says, 'I don't like to do that wit' you, baby, but you make me 'cause you won' do what I say.' Well, that's music to her ears, when a woman's got that psychology. After the whippin', they usually get in the bed, and things go along until the next ass-whippin'.

"With a ho, it's not like that. After she's taken a whippin', she sees herself as havin' to double her amount, triple her amount, to get out of that doghouse and get in your good graces again. With some ho's, I think they want the pimp to whup 'em, because they feel guilty about bein' ho's. If they can get you to stomp 'em, they can say to themselves, 'He makes me do it.' "

Pimps, he readily admitted, beat up their women. "But it's not like you came 'round with nothin' else to do, and just to pass time, you start to hit on 'em. Ho's are very rebellious women, very challenging women, and they are brave. Ho's is some brave motherfuckers! The one thing about a woman that isn't true of a guy, she's *dangerous.* I know men that got women that will go kill for 'em."

He thought it would be fair to say, he added, that beating your whores was a part of old-style pimp psychology that was "passing out."

Yes, he had beat up women who worked for him: "I had this ho, my buddy told me she was holdin' out on me. I sent another buddy over with twenty dollars to check her out. She gave me ten. I got her down buck naked and kicked her ass. I wanted other guys to see me as a real down pimp, that I wasn't a guy you could say about him, 'You think you be pimpin', but you really be sympin'." I did, I kicked that woman's ass, an' I told her, 'Bitch, don' bring this on me no more.' The hold," he said, pointing to his head, "is in here.

"It came from the git-go. It's in how you cut into a woman that first time. It's givin' her that confidence in herself and in you. See, you don't go get you a gal who's been a ho on her own all her life, and then try to drive her into givin' you her money. When you got a good moneymakin' ho, you got a girl you done raised yourself, a girl you *hand* raised. You, to her, are the basic thing after God. You are the only thing she knows as the basis and means of life and existence itself. But it always comes back to that thing that makes a husband give up his money to a wife: 'We're in this together. This is for us.' To keep it that way, the pimp has to take care of business. These so-called 'gentlemen of leisure,' they may have magnetism for their ho's, but when it comes down, they don' git respect.

"Things," he said, "happen to those gentlemen of leisure. They get themselves killed, for one. Then, I know pimps have had ho's leave their ass in some hotel, robbed like a motherfucker. They take the pimp's jewels, all his cash, hit the highway in his car. Then, you're really bad off, because when a pimp comes walkin' out of his hotel room with nothin' but his undershorts on, his ho's gone, his car gone, then he really has to hustle to get his thing back together.

"Or, his ho's get ripped off him."

I asked how that was done.

"One way is you just give an invitation to get on your team. You know: 'I been hearin' that things ain't too cool for you on your team.' Mebbe she sees your girls laid out in the best of shit, hears 'em sayin', 'We're gonna go to Las Vegas for the weekend. We gonna go to Mardi Gras.' If the ho don't have that kind of thing jumpin' off, and she gets that invitation, she's gonna leave him. That's one way.

"Losin' a good ho is like losin' a good job. You broke 'em in, you schooled 'em, they already know how to get down. You put a lot into educatin' a woman. Clothes, hygiene, makeup, small talk. How to present herself.

"There is just no doubt that ho'in is part show business. But a really good ho, she got a lot of natural game to her, and a lot of the stuff between her and a trick is spontaneous. She jes' has that feel for, 'Would it work right now? Would it go down?' A good ho has a high degree of con." As does, he added, a pimp.

"I could always cut into people, all my life. For some reason [with] my face, my makeup, people don't get alarmed right away. An' I can just let somethin' roll out and then pick my rightful spot in it. You play on that ability. You play on whatever's your strength. The things that you know you don't do well, you stay away from them."

I asked what, as a pimp, he didn't do well. Looking out the restaurant window, he nodded toward a group of young, uniformed men. "Like I don't like to be messin' with those sailors. With sailors you're gonna have some that get drunk and try to take 'em some sex. A pimp has to be knockin' those sailors out. But it's not just sailors that do that, either. Don' get me wrong. There's tricks out there whose specialty that is—trickin' a ho for free or for less than the amount. But those kind of tricks are on the lower level."

He sat back in his chair, portfolio on his knee, and drew tight circles on one side of his legal pad. "One thing that's said in the game, 'A ho ain't really a ho until she done been ripped off. Had to give some sex up for free because the trick wouldn't pay.'

"Ho's are just like you. They got things people never suspect 'em of. They got grandmothers, little brothers. They get birthday cards in the mail. They got toothaches. They got the flu. They got preferences.

"There's all this lay-on-the-couch stuff about why women do it, about the shame, the guilt, the heartache and sorrow. But there's a lot of fun to it. There's material gain, seein' stuff, bein' places, meetin' people.

"But a woman's not really a down, committed ho until some trick rips her off and she git up and go back out on the street and start callin' her up some tricks again."

A pimp like himself, a "pro pimp"—"one for whom the association with women is his primary source of income"—is, he said, "fast becoming a dinosaur."

"Drug guys, especially with the crack—it's created a glut of unsupervised prostitution, or what we call 'renegade ho's.' Or a lot of just sittin' around givin' up sex for drugs."

The old-style pimp, who roughed up his women, used them to do his housework, take his clothes to the cleaners, do his shopping, roll up his hair; that "style" pimp, he said, is also fast dying out. "Ho's and pimps change along with ever'body else."

He has no idea how many pimps work in San Diego: "In terms of number, nobody goes out and takes a toll. An' there's different ways to count who's a pimp. If a guy's a dope fiend and, to get his money to cop dope, he's got a dope-fiend woman with him, and she goes out to get the dope, he's pimpin' her. But he may not count himself a pimp.

"There are big pimps that come through here, because it's a vacation town, a recreation town, a travel town. You know they're here because new ho's are in town. Ho's can be very sociable. They cut it up with each other, seek each other out, have conversations. So it's, you know, 'Hey, we jus' came in from so-and-so.'

"But it's not a town where you have enough natural cover to do any kind of grandiose pimpin'. Take, Monday nights and Tuesday nights, it's dead here. You've got to find a place where it's jumpin', every night. This is too small a town. For instance, you couldn't pimp a hometown girl here."

What makes it a good place to work is that "it's a military town, a retirement town. An' nobody buys sex faster than soldiers and old men. When you look at the scope of society, who would want to buy sex? Who would be in such a hurry that they wouldn't go through the normal process of meeting, of talking, of dating? Sailors, military, because they've got a certain amount of hours to get off the ship, get laid, get dressed, get drunk, and get back to the ship. Old people, they got no time either. They're single, or them and their wife haven't had sex in years. He really lives in a house behind the house. He slips out every once in a while and spends him a hundred dollars to be with Lola."

What his women earn varies, week to week. "Sometimes I have a situation, one of my girl's tricks aren't around, and another's is. So one week might be bigger than another." One of the women is his main woman. "We been hooked up together most of four years."

A four-woman stable is the largest he has had. "That was in L.A. But we wouldn't just stay in L.A. We'd get on the road, go to Denver, to Reno, to Vegas, get us a couple of rooms, work the lounges. Before that, when I was first startin' out, sometimes I'd be carryin' three girls, and we'd do this thing, we used to call it the ol' ten and two: 'Two dollars for the room and ten dollars for the girl.' All that happens with that is, you go an' get a room. It might not be, back then, but an eight-dollar-a-night room. The girls trick out of the room. You be downstairs on the street, shillin' for 'em. When you're not workin', you're usin' that room.

"It was makin' me crazy. There's a great drive between ho's to outdo each other, and there's a lot of bitchin'. There's a lot of competition over the pimp. It's all the time, 'You like her better than me.' Or one of 'em won't want to work, and she'll say she's sick, and the other'll start screamin', 'She ain't sick, she ain't really sick.' It's jes' like some little kids."

His women are black. Most of his tricks are white. "White boys like to try a black woman, there's no doubt about it."

He had, he said, "worked" white women, but when black and white work together, there is "strain." "White women try too hard to fit in with black. It's pitiful.

"For sure," he said, "the money's not necessarily any better with white women. White girls that work Fifth Street don't make what black girls make that can work a hotel or do a convention. It's not your color, it's where you can work, and what kind of pimp you got."

He would not say how long he had worked "off a book"—a list of clientele.

"That means, you call me for girls, or you see one of my girls regular. You have some trust in me. You know there ain't gonna be no stealin', no police, no VD, no AIDS. I jes' don' deal with all that bus-station, skin-poppin' element, an' my girls use condoms.

"You see one of my girls, you ain't gonna get hit over the head. My girls is going to be properly dressed for your occasion, have some manners, not get drunk and sloppy. She's not gonna be somebody always lippin' off, bein' sarcastic, givin' somebody shit. There's gonna be some sweetness. The basic work, it's, 'You got Mr. Martin on Wednesday. You got Mr. Smith on Thursday.'

"On your book, that's where you get your odd little requests. You get your guy who likes to be sprinkled with baby powder, your guy who likes to have a girl twist up a towel, pop him with it. Those, they usually want to deal with one specific chick. Book guys . . . some of them may drop three, four hundred dollars. And with book guys, ho's and tricks gets to be friends. It can develop to a long-time thing. Just like"—he nodded toward me—"you go to your beauty shop, you see your same hairdresser every time.

"I get a call, someone I know, he will tell me he needs escorts. Or there might be one of those insurance-men conventions, and they have a hospitality suite, and you get 'em some girls to work that. Mebbe it's all the managers, or assistant managers in some company. But one of the guys for that group will have made that contact, and his group knows they're going to be served.

"Or some gangster with a restaurant—we got 'em here, gangsters. It's just no secret—one of those gangsters calls, says he needs to line up some girls. Or, some guy who's just springin' off a contact, he'll call me up, say he's lookin' to date somebody, or he's got people comin' in from out of town and needs ladies. For that kind of thing—a group—I'll get my girls together and maybe a buddy's.

"In group deals, I'll invite the guy to meet me for

breakfast to work out details. I make a point of dressin' conservative, bein' there on time. I show I'm dependable—all that. I want to make it smooth for him. An' with this approach, I'm makin' sure my girls is not gonna get ripped off. They pay me up front. And the guys the girls are with, they give the girls a tip.

"It's your belly that's gonna determine a lot of what you do. You try different business strategies. You stay away from stuff where you have a lot of chance of police. You work off your strengths. You ask yourself, 'What kind of environment is my girl strong in?' Mine are no good on the streets. Some girls are good at the street thing, they have a certain amount of wit about it. They can get out there and beg those tricks. So, there's them that do the street thing. But, it's too small a money. Same with the sailors. The money's too small.

"If it's a real slack time on the book, we can travel, or we'll stay around here, go to hotels: to the Grant, the Marriott, the Intercontinental, out to Mission Valley, to the Hotel Circle. Or you go around the airport, 'cause it costs more to fly than take a bus! But the thing is, you get into that bar atmosphere. An' this is where your stagin' comes in. It's in getting' your ho's ready to work. What you want her to feel is, she's gonna be a star.

"She get herself dressed just right. Little flash. Same when I go out with her. Like, for myself—just doin' whatever I do—I might get somethin' that costs five hundred, but don't have a five-hundred look to it. But, I go out with her, I gotta be adorned—I gotta stage myself. I go conservative. Your tie-and-hankie set. Some good cologne. But I add mebbe your alligator shoes. Somethin' that sets me off and says I'm not just some goddamn schoolteacher.

"We'll have us a drink. We're both radiating a thing. I'm radiating that I'm a pimp, and she's radiating that she's a ho. We're burnin' 'good times.' Men that are easy in this bar atmosphere, they know the signs. You're wearing your sign—those shoes. Tricks like that anyway, they won't spend four hundred dollars on a pair of shoes.

"We'll just look around. Make some eye contact. First

time you catch a guy starin', then it's your responsibility—the pimp's responsibility—to know how to come up with a conversation that apprises, 'Would this guy be interested in a date?' You don't have a lot of time to fool around with him. You jes' do some basic feelin', some, 'Say, how's the action in this town?' Mebbe he says, 'Don't know, but I like to play around a little.' And he looks at your girl.

"So you lock in on that guy; he's the guy. You let the conversation roll. Then maybe he'll say, 'I'm lookin' to date a girl.' So you do your setup story. Mebbe you say, 'I've got a buddy waitin' for me. I gotta go see him and pick up some tickets to a show.' Now, you've never defined her as being a ho. She's your friend. You just happen to be there together. You don't have to spell this shit out. So then you look at your watch, say, 'Why don' you and her set here, have yourselves another drink.' You get up and go. She's gonna do the rest.

"After you're gone, the guy may say, 'I'm gonna lay this hundred dollar bill up here. If you pick it up, I know you wanna go do somethin'. If you don't pick it up, tell me how much more I need to put down.' Guys in this atmosphere, they have some idea it's gonna cost 'em more than ten. But when the money's right, she's gonna say, 'Okay, baby, let's go do something.'

"A date lasts ten minutes, twenty minutes. While that's happenin', I'll go get my shoes shined, get the car washed, kill some time. It's not like havin' ho's out on the street. Then your primary responsibility becomes bird doggin', bein' right there, pickin' up the money, an' watchin' the girls. Those are the guys who get busted. This thing, it's her turnin' the trick and you pickin' her up after.

"Then you go somewhere and start over. Sometimes you won't get done until four in the morning. Mebbe after the last trick, you and your girl, you'll go have some breakfast. It's like anybody else then, come home from a day at work. You talk about what happened."

I asked if he felt contemptuous of the tricks.

"No," he said, "not at all. From a pimp's standpoint, a trick is a guy we think has got sense. He's sayin', 'Hey, look, here's your twenty dollars, here's your hundred dollars, your whatever. Jack me off, suck me off, do whatever you gonna do and I'm gone.' You can't say you did like it or you didn't like it or it was good, or it wasn't good. Or, 'Was it as good for you as it was for me?' It's just, 'Hey, here's my dollars. Any complaints you got, voice them to yourself. I'm back onto my business.'

"Deep down inside you appreciate one of the things that a trick has that you, the pimp, don't really have — to be with a woman, come, and then be through with it. A pimp has always got to be foolin' with women and dealin' with that magnetism between him and his ho's."

In larger cities there were regular pimp bars. But in San Diego, there was not a "pimp gathering place." Here, he said, "you just pass into the already identified slick spots, the hot spots. Where's it's jumpin' out."

He felt he was getting too old to enjoy "a lot of socializing" with other pimps. "The mentality of pimps when they are together is a lot like a locker room. All that poppin' the elastic on the jock strap, puttin' shave cream in your shoes.

"I remember a time in L.A., we were sittin' in a suite in the Marriott on Century, an' we put a trash can out in the middle of the floor, started makin' spitballs, seein' who can throw in the most, bettin' twenty dollars a crack. I jes' don' enjoy that anymore."

He didn't like the attitude "generated" toward women when pimps got together. "I seen pimps, when they together, spillin' hot coffee on they ho's, pushin' 'em in the pool. A lot of those guys just aren't sharp. They think all women is jes' goddamn fools."

He had been careful to tell me his was just one of many "niches" in pimping, that his business, while "well organized," was, comparatively, "nickel-dime." He made a living but he was no big-time pimp. He knew pimps who were, who operated "bordellos, whore stadiums." Some of the better of them, he added, "are women. Women can be very good at it.

They're more discreet. They don't have the need for all that ego and show shit."

I asked how he got into pimping. He shook his head in the negative. "That's that lay-on-the-couch kind of question. Jes' write that 'his uncle in Chicago hipped him to it when he was still a young man,' and you'll be writing the truth. You can also write, 'From the start, he was a very whorish boy.' Then write, 'The pimp I interviewed said he had never been totally committed to 'You have to work a regular job.' "

He thought he was "like a lot of ho's—a very rebellious person." He couldn't see himself having a boss over him, although making a living as a pimp, he said, is not easy. "You're always having to overcome the lazy atmosphere, and get yourself up and to work. There are dangers. There is always police."

He had never had a big bust of his prostitutes, he said, and he'd never been busted, not since he was a youngster. "You got to do a lot of stupid things to get busted. When a ho gets busted, nine out of ten times, you aren't there. It's only those rough-hustlin' street pimps that are out there. But then, there's the other side to it. I'm pimpin' an' I get shot. My ho's don' die."

One of the "gravest dangers": "You can find yourself mixed up with a woman who is a little bit too much for you. I've seen that happen, with pimps, many times. A buddy of mine got all hung up on one of his broads. Turned out she was a lesbian an' in love with some woman. He finally committed suicide. I know more than one pimp what has killed himself."

He has a son who lives in the Midwest. His son's mother, he said, "She didn't want no part of that pimp-and-ho life." Did he see the boy? "No, it's one of those mail-your-money-order, go to Toys 'R' Us and pick up something for the birthday, for Christmas kind of things."

I asked, if he had a daughter, would he want her to work as a prostitute?

"Hell, no. But it would be fair to say that I'd want my son to be a pimp."

At what age does a woman have to quit working as a prostitute?

"When she can't handle it no more. It's just like bein' a football player."

How long can you pimp?

He snapped his portfolio down on the table, sat up straight in his chair. "A long time."

How old was the oldest guy he knew who was a working pimp?

"I know a guy, he's in his sixties. Still pimpin'. Got him a BBQ joint, couple of little businesses, still runs a book on the side.

"In any profession, you wanna be good at what you do. Don't you? What determines how good you are as a pimp is if you've been able to get a Rolls and a nice house, a tailor-made wardrobe, a bank account out of it, and a couple of little businesses.

"But a pimp's report card never comes until the end of his life, until he says, 'Hey, I'm not pimpin' anymore.' Nobody writes your report card until you're through."

What kind of hopes, I asked, did he have for his future?

"You waited too long to ask me. Now, I just want to know I have a ho for tomorrow and some tricks be waitin' for her."

He wouldn't say how long he's been in town.

"Just write that it's livable, a place to rest. Write that California pimpin' is soft pimpin', that we're easy out here compared to the East Coast. There, whooo, it's git out on the streets—bam-bam—every goddamn night.

"So," he said, "why you want to write about a pimp, girl?"

I need money, I tell him.

CREATIVE IMPULSE

3

CREATIVE IMPULSE

Beauty shops did not exist in any numbers until World War I. Hairdressers reigned over what Peter Thomas calls "an old-style shampoo-and-set shop: a lot of chit-chat, a lot of gossip.

"Wives worshiped them. Their husbands razzed them. Women vied to be favorites. The pecking order shifted according to who made herself most stylish. The hairdresser heard everybody's troubles, knew who slept with whom."

One of Peter Thomas's male stylists reminisces about a hometown hairdresser he remembers—Mr. Meredith: "The day my father dropped dead in his hardware store, Mother telephoned Mr. M. to come to the house to set her hair. He came to the back door dressed in black and carrying pink roses. Mother cried in his arms. That was 1957. I don't know where he is now."

Since Vidal Sassoon stopped shampoo-and-set processing with heat, curlers, and chemicals, and began his Bauhaus form-follows-function school that cuts hair the way hair grows, shops like Peter Thomas's have set up all across the country, replacing shops like Mr. Meredith's. (Says Rita, "I used to be afraid of cowlicks. Now I let them do what they want.")

"Another opening, another show," says Mishell, gesturing across the room at her cast of colleagues in the shop. Paula, pale-skinned, with whispery Marilyn Monroe indolence. Kim—tanned, a bubblegum-pink mouth, pegged jeans, high butt, high heels. Big Richard, in lumberjack plaid ("I cut wood before I cut hair. I was tired of being dirty and alone."). Mishell, with Kabuki whiteface eyelids stippled black, burnt gold, gray—like bruises. Her black sideburns are spikey, her bang shaped to a droopy raven's wing. Mishell slides between tearful moppet in white tights and black patent maryjanes, to punk poet-manqué, to a look that prompted Big Richard to yell one morning, "Hitler! Mishell, you look like Adolf Hitler!" (Mishell had gelled the raven's-wing bang off her forehead.)

A fortyish woman pushes open the glass door, whispers her name to Patrick. Her jeans-skirt is wide-ruffled, matron-length. She has a fifty-dollar denim quilt-jacket (BIS—Paris, Beverly Hills), black turtleneck, Olof Daughters' clogs, challis-tie-printed Perry Ellis maroon tights. She droops, her eyes sagging, her hair burned out.

A skin-over-bones blonde watches as she waits for Richard to check her permanent. The regulars' "look" is synthetic, made (not born) beautiful, needing touch-ups and tune-ups but not the complete bodywork overhaul of the Beast class. And the art-for-art's-sake type, bred from bony, big-eyed mothers and straight-spined fathers, women with expensive skin and orthodontists.

"A good haircut generally is transforming," Peter Thomas

tells me. "Maybe not dramatically, maybe subtly, but transforming. Everybody has it." Peter sweats as he works, like a magus slaving over a hot piece of alchemy. "You can take somebody a little plain, even sorrowful-looking, and change them around. It's really incredible."

The recorded sounds on the salon's stereo are fed by the receptionist Patrick, who dj's twice a week at KALX on a show he calls "Audio Anarchy." Two days before Halloween, he stuck a plastic skeleton into his right earlobe. Blow dryers rev and gear down, high-heeled shoes clipclop. Peter's German scissors snick-snick. (Peter likes "more of a bite" to his scissors. "The Japanese are almost *too* smooth.") Water splashes down the brown shampoo bowls. The phone is ringing.

Aromas: piña colada protein conditioner, apple-green shampoo-suds, Peet's Major Dickason's coffee, ammonia.

"*Shampoo.* That movie," Peter says, "brought a lot of men into hairdressing."

"I've never seen *Shampoo,*" Tony, an apprentice, says. "But I always figured, there's thousands of women out there and a guy who's got any flamboyance can make it."

"It's not altogether untrue," Peter says, "that some male hairdressers are gay, but there are a lot of heterosexual males in this profession. Not only has the profession become more craft-oriented, but it's okay, too, to be a little less macho, to be doing hair rather than being out hoeing in the fields. But I know lots of people simply assume I'm gay. I've been told that.

"Male hairdressers take on female characteristics, just from working in a predominantly feminine environment."

Tony agrees. "You pick it up. You do little things with your hands, the way you carry yourself. Just like some women out there slamming a sledgehammer all day. She talks rough, eats rough, drinks beer rough.

"The clients," Tony says, "expect you to act a little feminine. A lot of people can't handle just a straight man working on their hair. They feel intimidated. You get somebody that's a little light in his loafers, a little softspoken, and they feel more relaxed. You can go to the back and cuss like a sailor. They're never going to know the difference."

Mishell snips a line around ears with her three-inch blade-worn Matzusakes.

"You should have a consultation first," Peter says, "before you even wet the hair. Because with a really good hairdresser if some sort of sympathy doesn't take place, it's really better for both parties not to go through with it."

The cutter runs fingers through the hair, lifts it up away from the face or presses strands down against cheeks, temples, asks, "How do you like it?" At the cutters' station apprentices offer the client Co-op cider, Peet's coffee, or Bolla Soave. Then the cut: sixty to ninety minutes. Marilyn says, "It's all the same motions, long hair or short. It takes about the same time no matter how much I cut off. It's all the same sectionings."

Each cutter-client drama, if it's a "take," arrives at the point of discovery—that Moment. "All of a sudden," Rita says, "the hair starts doing things and I get excited."

"Your nervous energy," Peter says, "gets all involved at that point. You get the shakes. *I* get the shakes. In the beginning I was terrified. I went through that for a long, long time. I've had cold sweats. When in the early part of your career maybe you've lost yourself—and it's particularly frightening because you've got to somehow find your way out of a maze and make it right—it's very delicate."

It's a rush, the turning point in the interstice. The client begins to look better. *Dénouement.* Marilyn says she checks "graduations"—a layering term. ("She's very technical," Mishell says, admiringly.) Peter checks for "accuracy."

Earlier I had gone to watch an assembly-line cutter at a walk-in fast-cut salon. I thought I'd see more transformations per hour in a franchise operation. I ended up seeing more hair falling much faster.

An old-time fast-cutter told me, "It's all basic box cut, basic one-length, basic wedge, basic layer cut. You start by making the top of the box, and then the sides of the box, and then the back, and then you cut the corners off. There's no attention paid to the type of hair, face structure, personality. It's factory work. There's no art."

I study the blower-warmed face of Peter's red-headed client, her hair taking on a sealskin sheen. Peter holds out the hand mirror. The redhead admires sides, front, back. Whispers, "Yeah." Her neck seems inches longer.

Haircut pattern books. Peter says, "I used to shun them. I'd think, well, it's not their face, not their hair texture. But now, actually, as I've gotten older, I've discovered the books *are* helpful. Even if it's unrealistic what a client wants, it describes the person's sense of themselves, lets me in on their personal fantasy.

"As soon as I see them, sitting down, I can tell what I can do. You just know, and that excites you. It sets your adrenaline going. There are certain people you just want to pounce on. You can see the potential. I can usually see to the end of the haircut before I even pick up the scissors. You just know."

As I listen, I am wondering, what does Peter see when he sees me? I feel that terrible chastening that any curiosity, sooner or later, makes us feel—a neediness showing.

"It's enormously self-revealing for some clients to tell you what they want—actually painful."

Mishell—Michelle Marie—was one of seven children of Roman Catholic parents. " 'Miss Hell' happened," she says, "when I went on this Catholic retreat and this guy couldn't figure out how to spell my name, right? because I'd changed, by then, how it's spelled from Michelle to Mishell. This was before I became a punk. When I started hanging out on Durant the other punks all had names like Johnny Puke, and so I said, 'Well, I'll just call myself Miss Hell. Why take on a pseudonym when I've had this all along?'

"Punk to me is now pretty well dead. People who come into Peter Thomas wanting something 'kinda punk,' it makes me bitter. Or wanting something 'kinda outrageous.' You're either outrageous or you're subdued. And then there are women who are real conservative, and they tell you like five times, 'I'm real conservative,' and I think, 'I can SEE that!' I'm *not* going to deface your hair!"

Shading her bruise-limned eyelids from the sun, Mishell sags. "When Richard said I looked like Adolf Hitler, I had to contain myself from throwing hot coffee in his face. It's from years of keeping it inside. The first time I threw something at someone, I felt fabulous.

"It was at Berkeley Square, which was a stomping grounds of mine. I was the darling there. These two straight girls were sitting, not bothering anyone, and there was this girl I knew from when I used to do Rocky Horror. She was with this guy who was real drunk and harassing these two straight girls. This guy had this porkpie hat on. So I said, 'Why don't you just lay off them?' and pulled the hat down over his eyes.

"His girlfriend tried to slap me. So I just stepped back and let her have it—threw my drink right in her face. And she grabbed my hair, and I started kicking her and punching her and pretty soon the security came, and they said, 'Whaddsa' matter, Miz Hell? We heard somebody's bothering you.'

"I said, 'She started a fight.' Well, I started it. But I said, 'She's been bugging these girls and pissing me off,' and so they threw her out. And the porkpie hat. It was great.

"I fell in love," Mishell says, "with this blond guy on a silver scooter. When I met him I worked hard at changing my image. I was a noisemaker, breaking bottles, throwing beer in people's faces.

"But I never got in fights back when I wore the spiked belt. Since I've subdued and call myself a mod, I got in a fight at The Clash with a big burly macho guy. He said, 'You're in my way.' Well, I'm too short to be in anybody's way, so I took a punch at him.

"When we were leaving, I went up and spit into his face

and said, 'I hope you fuckin' die in your car.' I figured that was the last punk show I'll go to. It's like the end of that whole part of my life."

In the ten-by-twelve-foot staff room boxed into PT's northwest corner, Heather, Paula, and Betsy squeeze hip-to-hip on the alligator-green plastic seat taken from a Chevy van. Heather slings her arm around Paula's broad shoulders.

Paula winces, leans over, and wriggles her blistered heel out of the three-inch leather spike, as the last of Jesse Colin Young's "Let's Drift Away" washes the staff room.

" 'My hair's his hair.' " The cutter comes through the door, squawking an imitation of the client just finished. " 'He likes it out on the pillow, spread out. He'll *kill* me if you cut it.' " Back to her own mezzo: "I told her, 'So don't tell him, he'll never know.' "

"Farrah Fawcett," somebody groans. "That woman ruined everything. I could cut FF's in my sleep. And Peggy Fleming."

"They shoulda' shot her, too."

"And Dorothy Hamill."

Kim yanks the canvas sacks of clean laundry away from the door to the bar refrigerator, reaches across brown bags, containers of yogurt, and two overripe bananas, takes out the green bottle of wine, kicks the fridge shut, reaches up over Betsy's curlicue blonde halo, and grabs a wineglass from the top shelf. "Boy," she tells the room, "they're startin' early today."

The timer buzzes. Betsy palms it and hauls up off the van seat, carrying a stack of aluminum foils she's been tearing off to wrap the hair she's highlighting.

Richard walks in behind Patrick, who wears a road-sign yellow shirt. Richard pulls his backpack out from under a blue slicker and a tan raincoat, rummages around in his scissors case. "Want to be noticed today, huh, Patrick?"

"Any male who sits in here," Mishell says, "gets fried."

Patrick takes the last chair at the red chrome dinette

table, unwraps a bologna sandwich, points at the *Girl Groups* book Mishell opens.

"Phil Spector," he nods toward the book, "locked his wife up for seven years in the house. Wanted her to sing just for him. In the shower."

"That's why I don't want money," Mishell says. "It makes you crazy. I'm going to become a famous bass player. I'm *not* going to become a famous haircutter, that's for sure. I mean there's some people I'm just a haircutter to, but what do they think—that I just stay home and read hair manuals? My God."

"Oh, cheer up, guys," Rita squawks. "I'm going to do a hair crime. Tonight. At the UC, I'll sit behind this long ponytail and cut it right off."

"The ones who are real neurotic about their hair, they can be a real pain. That's one good thing about this shop. We help people not to take their hair so seriously. Have fun with it. And whenever clients get really bad, we give them to Richard and he shapes them up. They're so glad to come back to us!"

"Some people," another says, "just sit there, diddly-squat. They put out ZERO. And sometimes you just can't think what to do with them. My mind just goes blank."

"People with long hair," I hear in the staff room, "are usually afraid to get their hair cut. They're not willing to let go of some of that hair. They're hiding behind it. Not everyone, but often."

"You can tell a lot about someone by how they look at themselves in the mirror. The worst is when they don't look."

"I used to be afraid to look at them. That's the hardest thing to overcome. To look at somebody in the mirror."

Spotlit under the west light, Peter sections hair, pulling two-inch clips off his turned-up lavender shirtsleeve and from the beltline along his jeans. The light from the window outlines his flat stomach under the thin-weave shirt. Not much more than a silk-stocking pulled down tight over a skeleton, 140 pounds fitted onto a five-ten frame, Peter has that look of men who eschew red meat. There's Peter, now, in the mirror; Peter out of the mirror, blue veins standing out across his broad forehead under a mossy furze. Both he and she are silent. He fixes on her reflection, then on her wet brownette hair. Giving the plastic spray bottle a whoosh, his scissors in hand, hair pulled down in strands between his first and second finger, both always held at the same angle, Peter dances in the direction he cuts, his expression the serious mien of an in-utero infant. (But later with another client, Peter will talk about the latest Nobel Prize-winning economist, about the client's new car.)

Peter, using comb and scissors, begins checking his layering, assuring himself that "there's lots of movement in the hair." The white towel square under his mirror is stacked up with two-inch aluminum clips. The spray bottle lies on its side next to a brush, two scissors, a comb, and Peter's teacup. The hair looks different—a shiny, moving cap.

Peter hands her the mirror. She looks from the right to the left.

After a few parting words and a handshake between them, Peter strides out, past Patrick, past the reception desk with its exhibition of bottles and tubes of Humectress, a Polymerized Electrolytic Moisture Lotion for the Hair; Therappe, World's Greatest Luxury Shampoo; Assure, A Botanically Fortified Shampoo; Ensure, Nature and Earth United; Re-Move, Nucleo-Protein Shampoo for Oily Hair; Cleanse pHree RePair.

He's gone to walk it off.

"Each stylist," Peter says, "seems to attract a certain kind of following. You can read a person from their clientele. It's a little abstract and hard to get a definition on. You can sense it. But I can't tell you just how it translates.

"I do a lot of therapists. I do an abnormal number of them. Each client has a flavor. So there has to be a connection. Richard gets glamorous types. Rita tends to have an avant-garde clientele, people who take risks, people on the edge. Over time you see, with each cutter, this clientele develop."

One of the cutters says, "A lot of people come to you because of what they see in *your* hairstyle. It clinches your clientele. But all your clients who come to you on a regular basis, there's something about them that's like something about you. Even though you have different lives and do different things, there's something that's connected. And working on these regulars, it becomes like a continuing saga. They're like friends. They sit down. I ask them what they've been doing since the last time. They ask me. . . . Some clients I just work on. That's fine. But with other people I enter into a long-term conversational relationship."

"You live on your repeats," Betsy says. (About sixty percent of clients are "repeats.")

"We did have the reputation," Peter says, "when we started out, of being sort of a punkish, avant-garde place. But it wasn't the full picture. We had simply allied ourselves with all that because it was the creative burst of youth at that time."

Talking in the staff room about Peter's cut, a cut that never quite "clicked," Betsy said, "Some hairdressers say 'Just do it, do what *you* think you ought to do. They're gonna like it when you're through.' But you just can't. I can't. One woman came in with one-length hair and I just cut a little line through the bangs, so little she could brush it back. And then the next time I was gone, and she came to Heather, and Heather cut a line right into her hair. She loved it.

"With each haircut we got progressively better. I just let her take her own time doing it."

"Again and again," C. G. Jung wrote in *The Psychology of the Transference,* "the analyst is caught up in a bond, a combination resting on mutual unconsciousness. The higher psychotherapy is a most exacting business and sometimes it sets tasks which challenge not only our understanding or our sympathy, but the whole man. The doctor is inclined to demand this total effort from his patient, yet he must realize that this same demand only works if he is aware that it applies also to himself."

"Many, many people," Peter says, "have had very negative experiences with haircutters. When we have our apprentices we teach them, 'If you can't listen, I don't care how technical you are. If you can't listen, we won't keep you.'

"It's a *serious* business. And if you change the way someone feels about themselves in a positive way, well, that's the goal of the whole works."

Eddie Cochran's "Ain't No Cure for the Summertime Blues" is put back through the stereo again; two lathered heads are under the shampoo water. Paula knows her client; they're far into a catch-up conversation. Richard shapes out a short-cut brunette who watches him in the mirror, flirts and grins.

Vicki, a big-boned, cream-and-roses-complected sizzle of a female. Vicki has just come back from a year in England, where she's had blonde dreadlocks attached with hairdresser's glue to her own naturally blonde hair (for thirty-five pounds at a London shop called The Antenna). The locks have been there since August, and to keep them, she's had to wash her hair cautiously.

Mishell takes two hours picking the fake-locks from Vicki's own, then assessing the damage two months has done, then cutting. The cut "catches." Mishell's scissors snick-snick, as she says, "I'd love to work in Germany, or England. They do really creative things."

Then she gets the shakes and goes to sit in the chair by the table where Patrick sat, three hours earlier, eating his bologna sandwich. She puts her black-booted feet up onto the second chair, ignoring the cigarette smoke packing the ten-by-twelve staff room, oblivious to the chat, the jokes.

> *Give me a look, give me a face*
> *That makes simplicity a grace;*
> *Robes loosely flowing, hair as free;*
> *Such sweet neglect more taketh me*
> *Than all the adulteries of art;*
> *They strike mine eyes, but not my heart.*

ADAPTATION

4

ADAPTATION

"When you went down to L.A. did you think that somehow working with the movies would change your life? That something would happen, that your life would become very different?"

"I thought it could be an amazingly happy experience, the opportunity to write movies. I didn't know how much abuse they would inflict upon you simply for the reason that you *could* write movies. That was the most despairing of all the impressions I received: simply the very fact that you have given evidence that you can do it becomes something they hold against you.

"If you can write a novel you can *certainly* write a

movie! That was my impression finally. And I tell you they see it, they spot it, and they are quick to grind their heels into your face the minute it becomes evident you might be able to do this thing. I cannot understand how so many people of considerable talent have persisted year after year in the movie business, how they keep going when they are subjected to so much in the way of pain and humiliation."

"Perhaps people do it for the money."

"I don't think there's any amount of money that can pay for what they go through."

We had taken a table outside on the Berkeley faculty club's western porch. Overlooked by trees, and almost empty now of diners, it was quiet. We sat inside a square of shade; I got out my tape recorder, then relented. We did some back-and-forth introductory stuff. He had come to California in the late sixties to teach at UC Davis, and then in the early seventies began to teach at Berkeley. He asked how long I'd lived in Berkeley. I said, "Almost five years." I asked how many children he had. "Three, two boys in their late teens and a seven-year-old girl." He told me he grew up on New York's Lower East Side, that his father worked as a barber. He had recently been interviewed, he said, by *The Paris Review*. He asked, "Do you know *The Paris Review*?"

• • •

The day before, I had sat in the sun on my fire escape rereading his novel, *The Men's Club*. I liked it even more than I had years earlier when it first came out. Meticulous and mischievous, it is narrated in first person by one member of a men's club, a college professor. The stories are about the members' various connections with women.

Leonard Michaels. His is a narrow face but not worn, and hardly lined, even at fifty. Jeans creased with an iron, rough curly hair, a worn jacket pulled on over a blue-green polo shirt. Despite the jeans, I never would have mistaken him for someone delivering beer to the faculty club bar. I glanced at my notes.

Leonard Michaels:

Professor of English, University of California,
Berkeley
Born 1933, New York City
Art Students League, 1943
High School of Music and Art, 1949
New York University, BA, 1953
University of Michigan, M.A., Ph.D., 1956, 1967
Author: *Going Places,* short story collection,
1969;

I Would Have Saved Them if I Could, short story
collection, 1975; *The State of the Language*
(with Christopher Ricks), 1981; *The Men's Club,*
1981

I had heard that Michaels was working on a new novel,
that he and his wife, poet Brenda Hillman, had separated.

He was worried, he said, about money. For money, he
had recently accepted a magazine assignment.

I told Michaels how much I admired the rapid pace of
the novel, and his ability to manage its unity of place—the
home in which the men's club meets—and time—one night.

"Yes, it's a real novel; it does everything that a novel is
supposed to do and it goes like lightning. Something happens
in the book that makes it possible."

"What?"

"The narrator, I don't know how to put this—he's not a
ventriloquist, which is almost always the case in a narrated
novel. My narrator talks for the men, approximating their
individual styles with his own voice. So that you're always
getting a flavor of the other characters without their ever
really speaking for themselves, and that gives the book a kind
of total unity. When, for example, you talk to somebody who
tells you a story about an argument, or whatever, you know
how that person will fall into an imitation of the other party
to the argument? And the narrator will often do this
splendidly. That's what I wanted from my narrator, to achieve
that in the novel.

"By the end of the book, the narrator is more enthusiastic, more concerned to become one of the men than he is to remember himself and tell his story properly. So he ends up telling this flat story."

I said, "In the book there is a story I particularly liked—Terry's story. Certainly *that* is in the movie."

"No, the best stuff in the book, they left out. A lot of the most extraordinary material was omitted because—" Michaels sighed, reached into his bag, and took out a battered pack of nonfilter Camels, tamped a cigarette on the wooden table, stuck it between his lips, and lit up. He showed more disappointment than satisfaction when he took his first inhalation. ". . . They really don't know better. These Hollywood guys, I tell you.

"The book is translated into twelve languages. It's sold one hundred thirty thousand copies in paper. It was adopted by every significant literary house in Europe. It didn't go to some mediocre publishing company in Germany. It went to Hanser. The same with Sweden, France, Italy. I know the book is pretty good in the eyes of very sophisticated literary people."

"Are you scared of the movie coming out?"

"Am I scared of it? Terrified. The prospect of the criticism just haunts me. I've thought of leaving town."

"It seems to me that you have been carefully laying the groundwork for making the public aware that you aren't serious about the movie, that you do not regard it as yours. . . ."

"If that movie is a mad success, I don't want any praise. If that movie fails, I don't want any blame. They took it away from me."

"What do you mean?"

"I was supposed to be there at the rehearsals and filming but they wouldn't let me. I understood. It was the hottest summer in L.A. history. People were fighting, slugging each other. They couldn't bear my criticisms at that point. They didn't want me around. So I sat in Berkeley and suffered and felt really hurt, badly hurt, and I thought they were cutting their own throats. How stupid can you be? Not to have the writer present *every* second. It's all writing. Every bit of it is writing. The director is writing when he tells an actor to play a line a certain way. When the cameraman moves, that's writing. By all means, they should do that. But they shouldn't deny me the chance to say something about it.

"No major studio in Hollywood would do the movie. I got a minimum amount of money for writing the script. Every actor who came in to work on the movie got very little dough. They came in on the basis of the script. They wanted to do it."

Looking around at the men in the faculty club, I could not help but believe that *The Men's Club* would have caused a furor among Michaels's professorial peers. I confessed that, wandering through the faculty club, I had concluded I could be watching a dramatization of a Dickens novel being played in modern dress. "What did your fellows on the faculty make of the book?"

"A lot of my colleagues disapproved of it very strongly. Some of them liked it, I suppose." But those who did not like *The Men's Club* had apparently not spoken their disapproval to Michaels face to face. "I just hear from certain gossip, that people repeat to me, what it is my colleagues say. It's terrible. It cracks me up. I feel sorry for them, having to live with me, as it were, and disapproving so strongly of the work."

Michaels waited out his laughter, as if the paroxysms that shook him were unpredictable lodgers who came in and went out with their own door key. After a few percussive bars, these throes of unbidden hilarity would begin to break into shards, then chips, of sound. When the last of the laughter had dissipated, Michaels spoke again. His tone had turned nasal, confident. "Of course, the book's a masterpiece, so I don't care."

"Are you tenured?" I asked.

"Yes."

"What do you teach?"

"English literature, moderns and Romantics. I'm doing a class on Shakespeare this fall. Undergraduates and occasional graduate classes."

"Do you like it?"

"Sometimes I love teaching. There are times when I'm wild about it, when I feel extremely lucky to have the opportunity to do this kind of work, but there are other times—times when I'm determined to write something—I can go crazy at the prospect of having to go to class in the middle of the day."

"You said you were worried about money."

"When you separate from your wife, life becomes terrifically expensive. I bought a house, a little house, to be near where she lives, in order to be near my daughter. I need that kid a lot in my life." He paused. "I got this house and I had to borrow a great deal of money."

"What do you and your daughter do together?"

"We just hang out. I have a beach cabin I sometimes go up to, near here. I haven't done that lately. Our relationship is largely verbal. We talk. How can I talk about this?" The question was addressed to himself. "As long as she continues to be affectionate, I feel all right about myself."

"Does being with your seven-year-old remind you of when you yourself were a youngster?"

"I didn't have any kind of relationship with my father that resembles that. He was a very very loving man and I just adored my father, but I didn't go places with him or spend a lot of time with him. Fathers were people who came home in the evening, ate a late dinner, read the newspaper, and went to bed."

"Well," I said, "those *were* the days before fathers were supposed to be 'sensitive.' "

"I think almost all of that is just bullshit . . . I've got to stop raving."

Michaels reconnoitered, seeming to go around to another side of himself.

After a moment he said with perfect gravity and the balanced delivery that comes after years of lecturing, "I think the opportunities for being a good parent become less and less available to us as we become more comfortable and adventurous and more concerned with fulfilling ourselves in this world. It's extremely hard work and it requires very serious dedication. I feel as if I've failed pretty badly. I'll never understand . . ."

"Is that your second wife? Your daughter's mother?"

"Third, sadly."

"I'm surprised that you married that many times. I would have thought you might have simply chosen to live with someone."

"This is very personal stuff we're touching on now," Michaels said. "I thought very highly of the women and I thought that things would work out well."

"I only wondered why you felt it necessary to formalize the relationships."

"Training, instinct, whatever. I met these women who seemed to me not merely desirable but to be women with whom I'd want to have kids. They struck me as having that kind of stuff."

"The right womb?"

"I wouldn't say that. They had qualities I would like to see reproduced in my kids. . . . And I was right about that at least. At least that worked out. I adore my kids."

Michaels proceeded to discuss couples: "A lot of people look great together. Some people as part of a couple look better than they would separately. The visual phenomena that marriage presents us with is, I believe, much more tragic than it is happy."

"Didn't you make that observation in *The Men's Club?*"

"Yes—it's something I have observed and have found enormously interesting—the way people look before and during marriage, when they get married and after the years have gone by. The shocking thing is to see one member of the marital couple after they've been married for years, to run into one of them on the street. You can almost see the toll marriage has taken on the spirit, especially (and even) when they look physically great. Because it sometimes is in itself the basis of a kind of disappointment; you feel a sort of disappointment in their physical well-being and the vast emptiness it seems to disguise, which comes through in that very physical well-being."

"And you got married three times?"

"Yeah. But I've always managed to stay in lousy shape. I'm not wrong about this. When I hear about their jogging and their eating right and so on, ho hum. You just know they're keeping in shape for all the other people they'll never sleep with. I mean what I say only partially literally. The metaphor is what I'm more interested in, that *is* more interesting. The dream that they imagine waits for them out there as long as they keep jogging, whether or not they literally do—the limiting factor, the thing they're running against, or away from, is the connection with a single other human being, the profound connection. The monolithic character of marriage remains always the abiding fact. And this is not an entirely bad thing. In fact, I believe it is the most important social institution and a very great necessity for the majority of people. However, this kind of sorrow that I am trying to point to manages to prevail, I believe, in the majority of cases."

"Was it difficult to move from one marriage to another?"

"Yes. I thought I was dying. I literally thought I was dying. When I began to live alone, I thought, night after night, 'I'm dying.' And it took a long time to begin to feel otherwise, to feel 'I'm just living.'

"I don't know if it's really been examined in the depth it deserves. There's a book by Bellow, *Herzog,* in which he does something with this. It's all about the state of mind of a man who has lost his wife to another man, and what's fascinating about the book is how the guy's anguish is disguised by a kind of exuberant intellectuality, which is only a species of insanity as far as I'm concerned, especially in his circumstances. The novel is fascinating for the reason that it treats the subject, the agonies of the man—for a change—when divorced, or what have you."

"Did you suffer like that every time?"

"In the most recent separation there was a long period of loneliness and grief, and then I had some good luck, which I don't think I ought to go into."

"Are you able to work when you're that unhappy?"

"Not much."

"I heard that you've almost finished another novel."

"I'm into it. I've got a ways to go. I'm writing various things, all at once. There's a movie, but I don't want to talk about it. I've got a collection of essays I'm trying to complete."

"What about 'academic' writing?"

"Scholarship? No, I'm not a scholar. I did enough to make myself creditable, and I try to read what I think is relevant to what I'm teaching. But I am by no means a scholar. I don't live in the library and I'm not inclined to be a scholar. I just read a lot."

"You said you read art criticism."

"Well, I always have been interested in art, as much as I'm interested in poetry. I went to art school, the Art Students League in New York. I used to imagine I might be a painter."

"You would have looked good at it."

"I wasn't good enough."

"No, I meant you would have looked good doing it."

"That would be the worst fate in the world, to look like you should be doing it, but not really be able to do it. I've had friends who were like that, some friends who were really great looking and totally dedicated too. . . . I shouldn't go on about this, they're still around . . . but without the gift, all they lacked was the gift."

"Some people," I said, "really look like poets, for instance."

"Isn't that sad? That's the worst thing, to look like you're the person who should be doing this work, and in fact lack the essential gift for it, to have every other attribute but that. There are some poets who really look like poets and are really terrifically good at it—contemporaries like Mark Strand, W. S. Merwin."

"Do you read new novels?"

"They're sent to me by publishers, and I try, but I so rarely have enough time. In some periods I read a lot of poetry, then there are periods when I read a lot of fiction, then essays. I'm sort of a promiscuous reader. I read very widely and in bulk.

"The Bible; I read the Bible." He quoted from the Book of Jonah: "He was exceedingly glad of the gourd." He repeated the line. "I like all those *g*'s," he said. "They're magnificent. They give to you the interiority of Jonah, his state of being and feeling at that particular moment when God makes a gourd grow to protect Jonah from the sun and the wind."

"Do you socialize much with writers?"

"I know a lot of writers, and I sometimes socialize with them, and if they happened to be a great friend before the consideration of being a writer, then I socialize with them. It's not often that I talk with them or anybody else about my major literary concerns. It's so terribly personal for everybody who is concerned with literature. You can't allow yourself in literary company to go into your likes and dislikes, your literary needs, your profound interests, for fear of jeopardizing a friendship. You can't because everybody has something at stake, and what if you sit around praising such and such a poet who represents to them the antithesis of their own work? So, the minute you have to begin to exercise that kind of care and consideration, then all real conversation is over. From then on, it is politeness rather than conversation. And I have very little time for politeness. In fact, I have virtually none. I *love* to talk."

"Do you ever talk about what you've read?"

"I do. It's mainly the case that I talk about it to students and to various friends who have nothing at stake in a literary way, or else their interest in the literary world is in no way competitive with mine. They might be critics, or literary historians, as opposed to being novelists or poets. There's too much risk when other people have something profoundly important to them at stake. If you watch what you say you can't even talk. Well, that's how I feel anyway. There are occasionally people you run into who feel exactly as you do.

"People are so terribly intimidated and warped by prevailing opinion, that, for example, if you want to talk about a big-deal poet, some reigning figure in the poetry world whom you don't think highly of at all—in fact you may not even think he's a poet—you wouldn't dare say it, because here are all these sycophants running around who are knocked dead by this guy's work, and you know in your heart it's no damned good at all. So what can you do? You just keep your mouth shut and try to get through the five minutes you're going to spend talking to that person. And then you go your way.

"The people I know who *are* literary people with whom I *can* talk very very freely, and say anything I want because I am sure they think, feel, the same way I do about virtually everything literary, they tend to be in the South. To tell you the truth, they tend to live in places like Alabama, where literary values are pretty much the same as mine.

"The South is the most truly literary part of America. When I say 'truly literary' I mean that people who are not directly concerned with literature would have the same view I do, people who work as lawyers, even farmers; I have the feeling they would feel rather the way I do about someone's prose or poetry. In that sense I think it is the most truly literary part of America. In New York or San Francisco, I would hardly ever expect that to be the case. There the person who is not steeped in the literary world would have opinions shaped by the newspapers and magazines, which are virtually never my opinions.

"New York City—it's ferocious there in regard to matters of taste and judgment, and so much of it is what I take to be manufactured in just one or two centers of publication. That is to say, the kind of opinion you discover in New York is hardly ever the kind that comes from a person, an individual person walking on the streets who has his or her own life concerns within which judgment and opinion are inextricably connected. Opinion in New York is not very existential, it is all very *manufactured.* I come from another place in the literary world. My views, I believe, are something that come directly from who I am."

"You praised the actress Stockard Channing, the wife of the man who hosts the men's club. So it seems that there are some aspects of the movie with which you are truly pleased."

"Well, yeah. I think you'll get your money's worth when you see this movie. I think you'll laugh. You'll be watching a Hollywood version of serious human matters. But only Channing achieves what I wanted. She is only on the screen for three minutes but she conveys a kind of miracle of intimacy.

"She did what was in the words. She found it. She's obviously a very intelligent woman. In just a few seconds, she achieved an intimacy with her husband on the screen, which was wonderful. She did it in a natural way and at great speed. I wanted something similar with these guys [Frank Langella, Harvey Keitel, Roy Schieder, and Treat Williams]. They're all stars. They can carry a movie by themselves. So what they did was terrific in this way and that way. But it was like an all-star basketball game instead of a real game where the guys are all together and serving some larger idea, which was in the book I think.

"Stockard Channing comes along and does that. She seizes the whole idea of the movie in every breath, every gesture, every time she moves. It's what I meant, it's *just* what I meant, she gets it more right than I did.

"Perhaps I shouldn't be so amazed that she should do that well. It's just that . . . I *know* she's a terrific actress, that isn't it. I was amazed. And I was *relieved;* I thought, 'My God, this is proof, this is all the proof I am going to get that this could have been a movie that I would have thought was great. This could have been wonderful.' If everybody had been willing to serve the idea, you see, instead of serving themselves . . . but that's something you can't really say to an actor—at least I don't know how to, especially when the actor is very good, as all those guys are, and in a way very generous, willing to do this thing for little money and so on. So I am bound to them by gratitude.

"Nevertheless, I wanted something else on that screen. I wanted intense consciousness of other people in the room, not demonstrations of individual flamboyance."

"Something like *My Dinner with André?*"

"Something like that, except I thought my basic material was much better. I would have loved it if that guy Wally Shawn had been in the movie. I proposed him as one of the actors, but Hollywood wanted younger guys. I was dying to get him for the movie, but they wouldn't listen to me."

"What *are* you going to do on the night the film premieres? Will you really hide out?"

"There's no *place* to hide. I just hope people will respond to it in the way they respond to all movies, that they will forget there was a writer. Of course, I haven't seen the finished movie, only rough cuts—the *approximately* finished movie, without sound."

"How, then, do you know it's so bad?"

"I don't know. My impression is that people will definitely get their money's worth. But it's not mine. I feel as if it was taken away from me, and they ran with it. And I wish them a lot of luck. It certainly would not make me feel bad if it succeeded. But I do feel distanced, and it was inflicted on me. Do you know what I mean?"

"Not really."

"They pushed me away."

"Did they not like you?"

"Oh, no, it wasn't that. Things were so tense and I was so critical."

"Were you rude?"

"No, never, never! In one case I even spoke into a tape recorder. I repeated everything I'd thought into the tape recorder and the director carried it to the actors. The actors seemed terribly sensitive to anyone watching the rehearsals aside from the director."

"Had you ever been in that kind of world—Hollywood, L.A.—before?"

"No, and I don't think I'm made for that. I'm high strung. My concerns become so absolute, they eat up my life. The idea of doing the movie seemed more exciting to me than anything in the world. And then it was all slowly turned into some kind of terribly poisonous experience when I was denied access to the production."

"What do you mean by 'denied access'?"

"I was actually barred in a way from the rehearsals. I was told not to be there. When they started filming I was also encouraged to stay away. A little bit they did up here, in Berkeley. That, I watched. By the time I was called down there to see the rough cuts, everything had been done. What there was to work with was very limited."

"What did you do then?"

"I cried."

THE BUS FROM L.A.

5

THE
BUS
FROM
L.A.

Benny was a long way from home. Only ten days earlier he had stood shivering under a gray New York City sky, his big bones cold. Now, huddled in line to board the bus from Los Angeles to San Diego, Benny said, "Ten years ago I climbed off the bus in Manhattan from down South. I kneeled and I *kissed* that ground."

In California, his hands and feet had warmed up but he missed Manhattan and the garment district, where, for seven years, he sewed collars on raincoats. Heaving gears and shuddering, the Greyhound bus pulled out into the downtown streets of L.A. Benny said he missed New York, "like a mama misses her baby." Someone who got off in L.A. had left a brown paper bag on the seat in back. Benny stuck his big hand into the bag. He withdrew an unopened sack of pork rinds and rattled it, then lifted out half of a Butterfinger chocolate bar.

"I don't eat rinds," he said. "They breaks down your teeth. An' I don' eat sweets, neither."

He opened his jaws wide. Gold flashed in the dark gap of his mouth. He closed his jaws and drew down his full bottom lip and pointed with a pale fingernail to gold dots set into his front teeth. What had brought Benny west—cramped in his bus seat through Pittsburgh, Columbus, St. Louis, Amarillo, Flagstaff, Phoenix—was his boss's heart attack. "He died," Benny said, "and then his wife fire me. He trusted me. I had keys to the whole place. She what give him that heart attack. She a *pure* devil."

The Greyhound swayed along I-5 from L.A. to San Diego, filled to capacity. From Portland, Oregon, to San Diego, the bus trip lasts twenty-eight hours. Coming in from Dallas it takes thirty-three; Boston to San Diego, three days.

Benny talked about all the devils he'd known. The first was his father, a white man he'd never met. When he was ten, Benny's mother, black and part-Indian, died in childbirth. No one in his family wanted him.

"They thought I was retarded. I got took to an institution. The officer that drove me there, he said, 'We're jus' taking you where some nice boys and girls are.'" Benny laughed. "To me my family is no family. They jus' meat." Benny's throaty voice rose when a portable radio blared one seat behind. A white-haired woman grasped the last seatback and waited her turn in the restroom. The bus honked as it idled, suddenly lurched ahead, then slowed again, blocked repeatedly in L.A.'s late afternoon traffic. Benny said he stayed in the institution until he turned eighteen. He never learned how to read or write. "Not even the alphabet. Not no more than to sign my name. It's a hardship. After I got moved into New York, I tried ever'thing to learn to read. I went to the Red Cross, to the board of education, to the welfare. But I can't read nothin'. It hurts me. A lotta' parts of life all be dark to me. But I understand the basis of life."

Benny's long legs are cramped. When the aisle empties, he thrusts his high-polished boots out into it and stretches his huge frame with a sigh. He said he was six-foot-five and 220 pounds and his red velour shirt was size extra large.

He had drawn out his savings and come to California after he got fired, but after five days in L.A. he did not like the state. He visited friends of friends. "They had nothin' but water in the refrigerator. That's pitiful. An' L.A. peoples is very country, very rural. Not like New York where they be fast movin' and fast thinkin'. L.A.'s not anything like New York. For instance, there's nothin' in L.A. for peoples to make money out of in the street with except drugs. There's no lottery and no numbers." Part of Benny's travel money came from a lottery winning. "I had jus' two dollars. What can you do with two dollars in New York? I put it on a number and got seventeen hundred dollars . . . Whatever hits my mind, I jus' plays it."

What he wants is to go on "The Phil Donahue Show" to tell the nation "how the government misused my life." He would say he was not retarded. "I was scared. Because I got beat up at home. In that institution I growed up nex' to children who had big water heads and children who meowed and drooled themselves and dirtied. I seen some kids almos' killed. I seen 'em given the electricity. I seen 'em fed Thorazines like candy. I seen sex crimes. When the parents come to visit, I wanted to tell 'em. But I knew the doctors and nurses would git me."

"They say God answers prayers. When I was eleven the institution wrote my mother's sister to come get me. I prayed and prayed. But she never come. I felt I prayed too much in my life, too many nights, too many moons. Prayer never answered me."

"What I believes in is devils. One time life was very beautiful. But peoples' minds is changing for the worse. You can see it in the way they treats womens. They call womens 'bitches,' and I don' like that. A woman to go out in the streets needs a dog with her that bites and snaps. There is no more culture in life. They don' hate us jus' because we black. It's jus' that peoples always needs somebody to wash they underwears." Benny laughed and rubbed his broad knee with his hand. "Women, no matter what race, they always been a slave." He laughed again. "I think white peoples hates blacks and Jews because they know all the shit we done gone through and we're still standin' up and bein' strong. But we all made outa the same mud."

The bus was an hour from downtown San Diego. Benny apologized for talking so much. "I haven't talked to nobody in two days," he said. He looked out at hills and houses. He could see the ocean frothing up and the sun going down, orange on the breaking waves. "This all used to be animals," he said. He was interested in nature. "You gotta be interested, because nature's you. Many times in my life I wanted to die. But then I'd get out in the sun. I takes care of my body. I won't never let no one operate on it or give me surgeries." Benny rubbed his broad knee again. "God put me here solid. I want to die solid." He pointed to the hills rising above I-5. "I likes those mountains," he said. "We don' have no mountains in Manhattan. It's all look down at the concrete, look up at the sky."

When he got to San Diego he planned to go to the zoo, then head back to New York and take that devil woman's recommendation letter and look for a job. He'd go into buildings in the garment district and, starting at the top floor, he would work his way to the basement, knocking on every door.

The sun had gone down and clouds that piled above the sea turned orange on their undersides. Benny looked out to the land side of the highway, sketching a circle on the glass with his finger. "I has a life, but I don' have no future." He turned his huge head. "But if I *ever* learns to read, you can be sure I will write a book that is so true won' nobody not be able to believe it."

Inside the city limits, the streets were empty. Benny said, "Where is the peoples?"

The creaking bus nosed into its slot behind the

Greyhound terminal at First and Broadway. The bus frame shuddered and it all came to a full stop. The passengers stood up, still talking loudly enough to be heard over the engine. They were talking so loudly that their sentences boomed out when the driver cut the motor. They picked through the bins above seats and rooted underneath for sacks, packs, coats. Benny climbed down out of the bus and stopped, stamping on the blacktop. He took in a long, noisy breath of the warm evening air.

"It already be night," he said. The gold dots in his front teeth sparkled when he lifted his head and pushed through the narrow door into the terminal.

The squat Greyhound terminal stands along the line of Broadway tattoo parlors, topless bars, and game arcades. It is shadowed by high-rise buildings. Almost no one comes to meet arriving passengers. The newly arrived find the pay telephones inside the First Street entrance and dial relatives and friends, then turn back to the benches, pile luggage at their feet, and wait. Departing passengers enter the terminal trailed by people seeing them off. They carry battered suitcases, boxes, and plastic bags. Each adult ticket permits the bus passenger free cartage for two pieces of checked baggage, total weight not to exceed one hundred pounds. Bus travelers make luggage from boxes, using a Hitachi crate or a Bacardi rum or bran-flakes carton, and wrapping and securing it with rope. Some packers contrive handles from wire and dowels and attach these to the crossties on boxes. The heavier-gauge green or black plastic garbage bags and the lighter-weight white bags are gathered at the top and wrapped with string and used to carry clothing. Smaller bags go on board, larger bags get checked. Stacked around the feet of passengers, waiting in line and on benches, are rolled-up blankets cinched with belts, sleeping bags, pillows, backpacks, shopping bags, Styrofoam coolers and rigid suitcases from the hard-luggage era.

The small terminal is waiting room and marketplace, with a twenty-four-hour lunch counter, a gift shop, the always-closed and mysterious Stage Tavern, a side door into the Pickwick Hotel, and a game arcade where video games snap and beep even when not in use.

Mike Ryan is Greyhound's day-shift Pinkerton guard: he keeps order, answers questions, directs passengers to the YMCA and senior citizens' hotels, points out the Traveler's Aid telephone number, and settles disputes. Ryan came to San Diego from Springfield, Illinois, where he was a social worker. Management wants the area kept free of panhandlers, prostitutes, and street people. Duos of card sharks strike up games of three-card monte with naïve servicemen. "The management wants them out, too, so I watch for them. To be in here, the rule is that you have to have a ticket or be spending money." In the morning, right after the first bus leaves for San Ysidro and Tijuana, the terminal pretty much clears out, and he does a ticket check. He can tell street people from passengers, whom he lets doze. The street people he speaks to softly: "You have to leave."

On weekends, when warships are in and the sailors have shore leave, lines for the hourly L.A. bus stretch out from the ticket counter onto the sidewalk. Normal traffic through the terminal is sporadic.

Over the loudspeaker a voice announces in English, then Spanish, that a departing bus is ready for boarding. Benches clear rapidly and a line forms at the designated door, and then the benches and the black plastic TV-watching chairs (twenty-five cents for fifteen minutes) start filling up again with women, men, and children, boxes and bags piled in semicircles around their feet. Many bus passengers are smokers. Many light fresh cigarettes off butts, several deftly roll cigarettes. A stout woman asks another, "Honey, how 'bout you give me one of them smokes?" pointing to the other's pack of filtered Camels.

Few people read. Most kill time idling: stroking hands, tapping fingers, staring. Older women prick at small squares of needlepoint canvas or crochet. Their reddened, arthritic hands are circled with colored wools. Crochet hooks flash. Women talk with other women and men with other men. If a man sits down by an older woman, she pulls her skirts in closer under her hips. When strangers stride by, older women grip their purses.

Street people ramble in from Broadway. They talk in conspiratorial voices on the pay telephones, or deposit three more quarters into storage lockers. In-transit passengers respond to their presence by pushing a foot down on luggage. Young mothers grab children tightly around the wrist.

The terminal's interior is decorated in a nautical theme with ship's ropes, life preservers, anchors, spars, portholes, and paintings of ships at sea. The gift shop is called the Gift Port Galley. The windows are stacked with button-eyed bears and plush stuffed dogs. Colored lights twinkle above the beeping video games. A shocking-pink vending machine vends helium-filled balloons. The terminal is like a carnival sideshow the morning after.

"Maybe they want to give us a sense of adventure," says Rassoun, head of a local reggae band. He sits on a bench waiting for his Jamaican drum to show up in the hold of the next bus. The drum had not arrived with him from Santa Cruz the night before.

A bus ticket from Los Angeles to San Diego costs $12.60. A plane ticket can be twenty-nine dollars or thirty-nine dollars. An Amtrak ticket is seventeen dollars. Most people ride the bus because they think it's cheaper, although on longer journeys a skillful travel agent might secure seats on planes that would cost not much more. People coming through the terminal have plenty of time and little money. They look poor. By middle-class standards, their clothing is ill-cut and carelessly sewn. The fabrics are sleazy. On younger men and women the clothing is intended to look sharp, even chic. But the polyesters and plastic leathers, and the botched tailoring, fail to emulate the high style intended.

Women and elderly people act humble, obsequious, often even fearful. They look cowed before ticket sellers and baggage clerks and shopkeepers, as well as bus drivers and broom-pushing janitors. Making inquiries, they look up with fear-filled eyes. The younger men, especially blacks, take an opposite tack. They taunt clerks and Pinkertons, daring their authority to offend.

After lunch the terminal falls quiet. A marine in fatigues lifts his Casio watch toward his buddy. "On my birthday it plays 'Happy Birthday' every hour on the hour."

In one of the television-equipped chairs, a man had pulled the hood of his sweatshirt up over his eyes and he snored and moaned, his head resting on the TV console. Doris, a cigarette moocher with a black eye, reached for a second cigarette offered by a woman. She broke off the filter and lit the rough tobacco with the flame of a kitchen match and peered from under a stiff black wig. "I'm forty-eight years old this coming month," she said. The other woman was trying not to have a conversation.

A pinched old man had slumped down at Doris's elbow. Thick white hair crested above his forehead. The cardboard tag tied to his bag read *Abilene, Texas*. He said to Doris, "Not hardly you ain't no forty-eight." He cackled, peering around Doris's bulk to say to the cigarette donor, "Don't believe her. She ain't gonna be no forty-eight. Not never again."

Doris frowned and drew up straight the two hundred pounds she carried on her five-foot frame. She breathed laboriously, her bosom heaving, breasts rising out of her black leotard. Her flowered skirt was cinched with a wide plastic belt. She had drawn a cupid's bow mouth inside her own fuller lips. Doris had no teeth. Her eye and cheek were lavender and yellow-green. Doris addressed her growing audience concerning her swollen eye: "Got socked with a fist." She made a fist and raised it.

From a town outside Redding, California, she had taken the bus down south. She had come to stay at her mother's, "to get help," and was waiting for her sister to fetch her. With babyish, lisping enunciations she said in her rough voice that her boyfriend in Redding had beat her up two nights ago and smashed her six-hundred-dollar dentures with a rock. "A big wock," she said. "Ve-wy big." In retaliation, she had poured a cup of sugar into the gas tank of his Toyota pickup.

Socorro thought she had heard everything in the years she bagged groceries in an East Los Angeles grocery, but she clucked and shook her grayed head slowly as Doris told her story. Socorro explained to the elderly woman next to her: "I don't regret not marrying. Not ever. Now I have my own little apartment in Los Angeles, and when I wake up in the morning, it is easy for me. I fix an egg. I do my needlework." She lifted the square of needlework up and showed off the owl with its yellow eyes. "And I watch my programs on television. It is less trouble for women not to be with a man."

Doris had not had teeth since she was twenty-three. Socorro overheard the phrase "a pool of blood," and shook her head again. The elderly man cackled. While Doris detailed the extraction of her teeth, he rolled his bloodshot eyes and scratched at his trouser legs.

The dentist had given her false teeth that would not "hang in right." But this pair, she said, "these that got beat? They were so good." Her battered, rubbery face fell in mourning, and she said it once more: "They were *so* good."

An older woman, blue-haired and prim, leaned around the man to listen.

"I shoulda' *sued* his ass," Doris said, then asked her audience, "Shouldn't I?" She didn't wait for a response. "There I was, just a girl, twenty-three, and no teeth in my head." Doris began to sob, her plump, ringed hand covering her mouth. The woman next to her clucked.

"Jack's his name," Doris said, "and he pulled me out of the motel court where he was for the night and he drug me aroun' some." Doris reached around to the underside of her bulging arm and twisted the flesh around toward her own face, bringing the bloody fingernail marks into view. "Then he grabbed out my plates from my mouth and put them down on the concrete and beat them to little pieces with a rock."

"Poor creature," Socorro said tenderly and looked at her needlepoint, frowning.

Doris looked over her shoulder. "Thank you, woman. I bet you," she said, "you all can't guess what I do for a living?"

No one answered. Only the elderly man, running long fingers through his white hair, looked squarely into her moon face.

"I'm a country-and-western singer," she said.

The man chortled and coughed. Socorro made a whistling sound through her front teeth.

"Sure as shit," the old man said, standing up. "You never been *no* singer except to yourself. Has she?" He looked to the others accusingly. Doris stood. She loosened the folds of her full skirt from around her jiggling hips and, mouth wide open, she cursed him.

"You old pisspants," Doris shrilled. She hissed foul words at him and spat toward his boots, then hefted her baby-blue Samsonite cosmetics case from the floor. Breathing stertorously, she leaned over to pick up her fallen white purse, then the matches, the compact, bloody balls of tissue, and dollar bills. With her rump in the air it seemed for a moment the old man might kick her.

Except for the old man, who remained standing, Doris's listeners all directed their eyes elsewhere. She waddled slowly away in her terrycloth slippers, her feet bare, her gait almost foolishly graceful. Doris swayed across the terminal's green floor, cut through rows of benches and passed the Gift Port Galley's lighted display of dogs and bears, the pink balloon machine, heading for the pay phones.

The four o'clock bus to L.A. was announced over the loudspeaker. People grabbed up their shopping bags and purses and suitcases, and struggled toward Door 2. Through the exhalations of exhaust pipes and the grinding of gears outside, the loudspeaker announced buses boarding for Sacramento, San Francisco. For San Ysidro, Tijuana . . . .

THANKS FOR THE MEMORIES

6

THANKS
FOR
THE
MEMORIES

Elephants form matriarchal family units. The Asian bulls—who, when they mature, go through periods called *musth* and can become violent—are isolated from this matriarchal society and have a kind of bachelorhood. The cows chase the bulls away from the herd and they are allowed back only for mating.

A pecking order exists among the females. The lead cow, the head of the unit, will tend to be the animal in the herd who has lived longest. Individual members of the herd are very close.

"Elephants who are dying, who are sick, they don't just die suddenly. They go down," says Alan Roocroft, elephant training supervisor of the San Diego Zoological Society. "The other elephants will try to motivate the sick elephant, to get it on its feet. They will try to get that elephant to want to live. The little males will try to mount it if it is a cow who is dying . . . not as a sexual thing or as a perverted act, but as a motivation for life. In a herd in the wild the elephants will stay with a dying member of the herd until he or she is either up and moving, or dead."

Because elephants are the most voracious of feeders among land animals, consuming three hundred to five hundred pounds each day of leaves, bark, branches, grass, and other vegetation, they must stay on the move to have enough food. The female lead elephant, Roocroft says, will know where, and in what seasons, to find food. "Her mother will have showed her, and her mother's mother before her. She would have been born into a family unit of six or seven elephants and would have remained a part of that unit for sixty, even seventy years."

For the first years, she would be with her mother all the time. "And there would be one other elephant with them, the auntie." The "auntie" and the mother come together by mutual agreement. Because the time of birth is, for the female elephant, a time when she is in the most vulnerable position, the two females will choose a place to give birth where the mother will be protected on at least three sides. "Sometimes," Roocroft says, "it will be a stream bed." But the auntie, he adds, "will *always* stand on the fourth or unprotected side." In Asian jungles a tiger will often track the pregnant mother and the auntie for weeks. "The tiger senses the animal is going to give birth, and if the tiger is hungry, it will attack. Because the auntie has stationed herself on the fourth side, she will be attacked first."

In contrast, the herds in captivity are entirely artificial, synthesized with members from different family units, different herds, even different subspecies.

•   •   •

The late Morgan Berry began importing elephants into the United States in 1952. He brought in 120 of them over the years and sold them to zoos, circuses, trainers, and private individuals. In 1962 he bought a female elephant from an animal dealer in Bangkok when she was six months old. She came to the United States in the belly of a Boeing 707, and Berry kept her until she turned two. Her name was Cindy.

In 1964 she was sold to someone in Nevada to serve as a children's attraction at a resort and casino complex under construction in Boulder City, a town thirty miles from Las Vegas. Before 1960 the 130-acre property, which included twenty acres on Lake Mead, was a largely undeveloped area around the Gold Strike Inn. Then the Gold Strike owners leased the property to a promoter who called it Fort Lucinda. He planned to turn the development into a large-scale tourist attraction, and Cindy was part of his plan.

Morgan's son, Ken Berry, worked with his father. He does not recall Cindy by name, but he remembers taking one elephant from Seattle to Boulder City, Nevada.

Berry was to deliver the elephant on payment of four thousand dollars. "I picked up someone at the Sands who gave me the check and drove with me to Boulder City." Berry was put up in a motel for a week. Part of the four thousand dollars included Berry's teaching someone to care for the elephant.

David Belding, a Reno attorney, was eighteen in 1964, Cindy's last summer in Nevada. Belding remembers her well. The summer of '64 he worked in a gas station from midnight to eight. Cindy lived in a nearby tent, and Belding would sometimes bring her to the station. Shiny things attracted her. She liked to take off Belding's watch, and he taught her to crush pop cans with her trunk. One night, Belding remembers, a drunk passed out on the seat of a trolley car on the property. Belding tiptoed to the sleeping man and put a pop can on his stomach. Then he led Cindy to the trolley. She grabbed the can. "The man sat up, took one look at Cindy, and ran," Belding said. "He never came back."

During the day Cindy gave rides to children. She was moved to a shed and was kept company by a billy goat. The temperature would rise to 120 degrees in Fort Lucinda, and Cindy had no shade. She collapsed several times. The humane society complained.

Norman Winnick, director of Tacoma's Point Defiance Zoo for fifteen years, was there in 1965 when a man in Nevada offered Cindy to the zoo as a gift. But the zoo had to pay for transport. All that Winnick knew about the elephant was that she was young, in good health, and had grown too large for her owner to keep.

Port Defiance had a "zero" budget for acquisition. "We were, back then, a roadside zoo with a few niceties," says Norman Winnick. Winnick contacted the newspaper and told his story. After the paper ran a front-page article, a local roofer offered to transport Cindy free in his new flatbed truck. The zoo shop built a crate for the flatbed. Money was found to fly Winnick from Tacoma, Washington, to Nevada to work with Cindy for ten days.

When Winnick arrived, Cindy was in the care of a man who called himself Jo-Jo the Clown. Cindy was about four feet high at the shoulders, four years old, and a little on the thin side. Dressed in her red velvet caparison that bore her name emblazoned in gold letters and wearing her diamond-shaped hat, Cindy often went into Fort Lucinda's small bar, a room that held gaming tables and slot machines. Winnick learned that because of her size, Cindy had begun to knock over tables. She had also become fond of maraschino cherries, using her trunk to extract the cherries from customers' drinks.

Winnick was not told everything. He did not know Fort Lucinda was in financial trouble, nor did anyone tell him that the humane society had spoken of its concern to Fort Lucinda's promoter. And nobody could tell him of Cindy's origins far from the sands of the Nevada desert. He just saw to it that she was delivered safely to his zoo in Tacoma.

"Cindy really became a star, and she was also really the first attraction, the first kickoff for getting support for the zoo."

When Cindy entered adolescence, Winnick tried to arrange with the Portland zoo to breed Cindy. But this never worked out. Winnick also hoped that after a 1977 bond issue, the Tacoma zoo could build larger elephant quarters and also purchase a second elephant. But by 1980 Winnick was gone from Port Defiance, and Cindy remained alone. She was the zoo's first elephant and its only elephant, and she paced her asphalt enclosure alone. She had one great friendship—with her second keeper, Rich Johnson, who assumed her care in the seventies.

• • •

An elephant's life in captivity is, of course, very different from its life in the wild. "In the wild," Alan Roocroft says, "an elephant will be moving at least eighteen hours each day. The feet, then, will take care of themselves." But in a zoo, elephants develop overgrown toenails and over-thickened foot pads. "The most important part of health care in an elephant's captive life will be the feet. An elephant cannot be kept on concrete, on rocks. She does not *live* on rocks. An elephant needs sand. An elephant needs Mother Earth."

Water, he says, is a necessity. "Not just for drinking, but for bathing and for recreation, too. Skin care, water and sand—mud—are a part of the elephant's day. When they get wet, they itch, and they need rocks and stumps to rub against. They need sand to toss on themselves."

The diet of the elephant in captivity has always been a problem. "People imagine the bigger the animal, the more you feed it, but this is not necessarily so. Basically, you give an elephant as much hay as she will eat. But you have to remember that, in the wild, eighteen out of twenty-four hours she would be moving. She pulls up a tuft of grass, or breaks off a branch, and eats that, and that tuft gets her to the next tuft or branch.

"Now, in captivity an elephant stands in one place and we throw hay to her all the time. This is where instinct, the gut feeling of a keeper must come in. A farmer can tell you when it's going to rain. Well, I can tell you when the elephant is not eating right, is not moving right. If she is not moving enough, she is getting too much food. So we must cut back her feed a bit. I would rather, always, give them a little less and motivate them more—achieve movement to that next branch, as it were.

"But," he says, rubbing his own fingertips together, "it is a fingertip feeling, a feeling that you get from an animal that tells you this.

"Elephants need touch. They need to *feel* other beings. Isolation, you see, it's the worst thing for an elephant. When they are isolated, their whole life is distorted. Add to that the inconsistency of human beings working with them, their lack of knowledge and experience of the animal, and then it is no wonder some elephants hit at people. A dolphin has the smarts to commit suicide when caught in such a situation."

Although children flocked to her and fed her the Lifesavers candy she so craved, approaching her on business grew increasingly problematic for everyone except her keeper. Because Cindy scared other keepers, Rich Johnson came in on his days off to clean her stall. She had become a "one-person elephant."

Tacoma's zoo curator said, "If something should happen to Rich, or if he would choose to work somewhere else, no one could get close to her."

When zoo veterinarian Mike Jones tried to tend to Cindy, there was trouble: "She picked me straight up in the air, and if Rich hadn't been there, I wouldn't be here either." The only way to treat Cindy was to tranquilize her, but that posed a danger to Cindy's life.

Early that summer of 1982 Point Defiance hired Roger Henneous, the senior keeper of elephants at Washington Park Zoo in Portland, Oregon, to evaluate Cindy's behavior, to "retrain" her, and to train keepers to care for her. Zoo workers have a healthy respect for elephants, and rightly so; although the public believes lions, tigers, and bears are the most ferocious zoo residents and circus performers, those zoo and circus workers who are killed or injured most often fall victim to elephants. Henneous's five days with Cindy were frustrating. At one point, after he tapped her on the nose with a training tool known as a bull hook, Cindy stuck her trunk through the bars and knocked Henneous to the floor.

Point Defiance then hired Richard Maguire. Called "The Hammer," Maguire breaks "bad" or "rogue" elephants. Looking on, zookeeper Rich Johnson sobbed. After five days Maguire's retraining ended — unsuccessfully.

• • •

Alan Roocroft: "You quickly learn what your own inadequacies are when you work with animals. If you don't, the animals will teach you. The frustrations take over when people can't teach an animal a behavior. I've done it. You feel like an asshole. My own inadequacy, you see, would take over. You just stand there, just before taking an action you know is not right. But you do it . . . and then you come back to yourself, and you say, 'What in hell *are* you doing?'

"You see people brutalizing animals. You see situations in which an animal is so frightened it will not come to its trainer. I have seen elephants, who have been beaten, cower. But twenty, thirty years ago? You could do anything. It was a given mode of authority — man over animal — that nobody questioned."

At least fifty male elephants have been killed in this country. Mandarin, a Barnum & Bailey circus elephant, is one of two males to have been hanged. Early in the 1900s Mandarin killed three men: a drunk who teased him, a trainer, and a stable boy. He was hanged with a ship's winch. *I Loved Rogues,* by elephant trainer George "Slim" Lewis, mentions the second, Topo, "hanged from a tripod made of huge logs when he refused to obey his trainer."

An elephant named Tusko died in 1962 at the Oklahoma City Zoo from an overdose of LSD, administered in the hope that it would calm him. The huge combative Ziggy, who spent twenty-nine years locked in solitary confinement at the

Brookfield Zoo in Chicago, escaped the San Diego Exposition in 1936 and took refuge in Balboa Park. But Hari, a male who came to the San Diego Zoo with Lucky and Maja (still residents there), is the only elephant to have been executed in San Diego. In 1945, after Hari attacked his keeper, the elephant yard was roped off and Hari was shot before the zoo opened for the day.

• • •

Tacoma's Metropolitan Park District Board met in October of 1982 and a letter from Roger Henneous was read. It said in part that Cindy was "by far the most aggressive, malevolent elephant I've ever seen. Why Cindy hasn't killed or maimed someone already is a complete mystery to me, but it is only a matter of time until she does so."

Tacoma zoo director Gene Leo told board members, "Several staff members have been hit, picked up, rapped, and thrown." Keepers had been instructed not to work around Cindy. He suggested three alternatives: sell Cindy; sell Cindy and buy a baby African elephant, which would cost from twenty thousand to thirty thousand dollars, including subsidiary costs; or hire a trainer to retrain Cindy at a cost of thirty-two thousand to thirty-five thousand dollars. Leo favored the last, although he told the board that only a fifty-fifty chance existed that the "retraining" would work, and added, "This is a very difficult decision, given Cindy's popularity in our community."

The board postponed its decision on Cindy's fate, but the elephant remained in the news. Although Cindy had never injured anyone to an extent requiring hospitalization, "mad elephant" stories circulated through the city of one hundred sixty thousand. So did the rumor that the elephant would be destroyed.

Allegations that Cindy had been abused in her summer's retraining appeared in Tacoma's *News Tribune.* Namely, that Cindy had been beaten with boards, jabbed with a pitchfork, stabbed in the trunk with a penknife, zapped with an electric cattle prod, and, at least once, chained by all four feet to the enclosure fence. Further: "It was learned that Cindy fell to her enclosure floor in exhaustion and remained there for four hours on one occasion and six hours on a second occasion, both during the same twenty-four hour period. The trainers were reportedly unsuccessful in their use of cattle prods, finally coaxing Cindy to her feet after her leg chains were loosened."

One source told the newspaper that the chains dug two inches into one ankle. Another source called the retraining methods "sickening."

There was ugly talk around town. A park groundskeeper told friends he had seen Cindy beaten with two-by-fours, that hay was tossed into her pen atop her excrement, that she was being starved.

Four days after the *News Tribune*'s article appeared, Tacoma's park board met again to discuss Cindy. One hundred Tacomans packed the room. While television lights blazed, twenty-three citizens gave testimony, both for and against the elephant. A keeper, who had filled in while Johnson was on vacation, testified that, "Cindy slammed me with her trunk, threw me six feet, broke my glasses, and I lost consciousness. That was the most terrifying experience of my life." Two citizens brought up the successful 1977 seven-million-dollar bond issue for zoo rebuilding. Cindy's photograph had appeared in the advertisements. Her new housing, promised in the bond proposal, was never built.

The directors deliberated and announced their decision. The board had resolved to consummate a permanent breeding loan agreement with the Zoological Society of San Diego. The provisions would stipulate that Tacoma's zoo own Cindy until she produced a female calf. Tacoma would get the calf, and San Diego could keep Cindy.

It would be a good deal for San Diego. Asian elephants had been declared an endangered species, and a breeding-age elephant cost thirty-five thousand dollars. Cindy would increase the breeding stock and gene pool for the planned Asian elephant breeding program. San Diego would have to pay only a six-thousand-dollar transportation fee. The weekend after the board met, Gary Miller, elephant trainer at the Wild Animal Park in San Pasqual, flew to Tacoma to visit Cindy. On his return Miller reported to the Zoological Society that Cindy was an excellent candidate for the breeding program. He did not believe she was dangerous, but only that she was "bored, for lack of companionship."

Among zoo personnel, it would have been unthinkable to make public comment on Cindy's "retraining." Zookeeper Rich Johnson, who had worked with Cindy for years, said he had been ordered by officials to refer all inquiries to the zoo development officer. He intimated that he had been threatened with loss of his job if he commented. Zoo employees do not discuss with outsiders the skeletons in one another's closets. Negative comments about other parks was simply "not professional."

Neither Henneous nor "Hammer" Maguire was available, but Mike Jones, the zoo's veterinarian, did speak to the paper in the zoo's defense.

Persons unfamiliar with professional elephant-training methods may view those methods as abuse, he explained, when in fact they are merely necessary applications of discipline. In answer to charges that the animal was struck with wooden boards, Jones told the Tacoma newspaper that Cindy was struck with boards only when the four-ton elephant attempted to attack trainers. "She's the size of a Sherman tank," he said. "You can't use your hand and expect her to feel it." About the penknife, Jones said, "An elephant trainer did use a penknife on Cindy only because no other elephant hooks were available. Her thick hide was not jabbed any deeper than one-quarter inch." Jones also admitted he had purchased and used the cattle prods himself; but they had little effect on Cindy. "She barely noticed," he said. "You've got to recognize how thick that hide is." To the charge that Cindy had been chained and left without food or water, the *News Tribune* noted that Jones replied, "Food and water were withheld on occasion in order to use nourishment as 'rewards' for appropriate behavior."

In a phone conversation, Roger Henneous did not recall that the *News Tribune* tried to contact him about the alleged retraining abuse. Henneous, who has been with Portland's Washington Park Zoo for fourteen years, said, "I don't pretend to be a trainer, just a keeper. I have no illusions about being an authority." Although at the Portland zoo Henneous is used to working with three bulls, he said about his encounter in 1982 with Cindy, "I never met a female elephant with such an in-your-face-Jack, impolite attitude." In his opinion Cindy was not vicious by nature, but was permitted to "rough people up" without consequence.

Asked if he felt uncomfortable about the allegations of abuse, Henneous said, "No. If I had been guilty, I would." He reiterated what many elephant trainers and keepers say: "The layman does not understand elephant training, or elephants. They are big, smart, and if they ever take it in their head to snuff you, it's all over.

"Had I gone into Cindy with a chain saw and a .22 and physically scarred her," he said, "*then* I would feel bad. But the simple matter is that if you start with an elephant at a young age, then you don't have to be that rough. But if you wait until an elephant is Cindy's age and size, there's very little poking, gouging, and thumping you're going to do that will injure it."

• • •

The "evil elephant" brouhaha began in San Diego after trainer Gary Miller went to Tacoma. Jeff Jouett, a spokesman in the zoo's public-relations office, received a call from the San Diego Associated Press bureau. "They had a story from Seattle," he says, "that Tacoma's zoo wanted to send us this vicious elephant." Immediately the sensational aspects of media coverage became overwhelming, with local stories calling Cindy "dangerous" and "malevolent" appearing. The story was picked up nationwide. "I backtracked," Jouett says, "and discovered that Henneous's statement was originally that 'under these circumstances, Cindy was dangerous . . .' et cetera. But for the sake of brevity, I guess, the qualifier was dropped. And at that point the Zoological Society trustees almost decided against accepting Cindy. They had heard so much about her being a killer that they were not sure they wanted her."

The board asked Miller to come before them to discuss Cindy. Satisfied with his diagnosis of her as "bored," the trustees voted unanimously to accept her.

After that decision, headlines read, " 'Dangerous' Pachyderm Finds Home," and "Brooding Elephant to Take up Breeding." Then, Jouett says, "I began receiving calls at home at night and throughout the day at work. Everyone wanted to know why we were taking this 'vicious' elephant. And with every story this 'vicious' reputation grew." Jouett's public-relations goal became twofold. He had to debunk Cindy's reputation as dangerous. Yet, he admits, he had to be careful "not to insult the Tacoma zoo. I truly believed the Tacoma zoo was doing the best they could on a limited budget."

Debunking Cindy's reputation was not easy. "Even after I told press people that Cindy was a victim of her past treatment, of being locked up in a small enclosure, of having untrained supervision, even after I would explain Cindy's behavior from an elephant's point of view," Jouett says, "people would not include those items in their story. The stories would always start out with that 'most dangerous elephant' angle."

Worse yet, media representatives wanted to be present when Cindy arrived in mid-December. The elephant trainer and keepers wanted no one there. They were concerned because Cindy had not seen another elephant for seventeen years. And she would have been jostled in a truck all the way down Interstate 5 from Tacoma for more than twenty-four hours, all the while chained, "but for different reasons than we felt the press would assume, given her reputation," says Jouett. The chain, he explained, would permit the trainer to move her and keep other elephants from pushing her into the moat around the two-acre park enclosure at her destination.

The decision was made: bring Cindy in at night, and don't notify the media. Jouett saw no way out. If Cindy did behave in a berserk manner, there would be no way to fully protect the reporters. And at night, in complete darkness, Cindy would be less stimulated by the strange new place.

The Tacoma zoo's director, Norman Winnick, also feels the "evil elephant" story got out of hand, that Cindy was not malevolent, only lonely. Left without elephant companionship, Winnick believes that Cindy tended to approach keepers as if they were also elephants. Winnick recalled that at the same time newspapers called Cindy dangerous, young children were still being held up by mothers to hand Cindy treats.

"Cindy would take these delicately with her trunk from their tiny little fingers. She was doing this up to the day she left for San Diego."

On the Friday before Cindy headed to San Diego, fifty Tacoma residents gave her a going-away party at the Tacoma zoo. They stood beneath a green-and-yellow circus tent, sipping hot cider and munching animal crackers. Stickers were passed out that bore an elephant sketch. People tied four bouquets of balloons to Cindy's fence. Cindy looked up at the balloons while she munched the fresh hay Rich Johnson spread in her yard. He seemed happy at her good fortune and understandably sad at her leaving. He would keep some small treasures to remind him: two of her baby teeth, the red velvet caparison Jo-Jo the Clown had once given Norman Winnick in Nevada, a bracelet made of her tail hairs. After seven years they were saying good-bye.

• • •

Roocroft: "You get a new elephant. What do you do? People say, 'Well, you beat it. Beat it into submission.' Well, that's bullshit. You have to bring these animals into the awareness that they are in captivity, whether they have been totally wild or come from another institution. They have to be shown that they are in your hands.

"The first step is to introduce yourself to the animal, to develop what my boss in Hamburg called the *appelle* ['the call']—teaching an animal that it is being taught."

If you cannot teach an elephant that it *is* being taught, then the rest of the training will be torture for the animal.

"You can either produce something very, very fine for both the animal and the trainer, or, if you are a thumper, by your own actions you can produce a monster: you will get an elephant that is nuts.

"Too many trainers begin their work with an elephant by visualizing a little man in the elephant's head. The trainer is trying to train, so to speak, *that little man.* When that little man does not respond—when the elephant does not do what the trainer has asked it—then the little man grows larger. And the harder you fight the little man, the more the human ego becomes involved and the bigger the little man gets. It becomes a contest of wills. This never works. What you have to do is to 'think elephant.'

"Working with elephants, I go for gut feeling. The animals are dealing with their instincts. Our instincts have been slowly beaten out of us. We have become a regimented machine. But the animals are dealing with their instincts. To work with elephants, you have to go with your own gut feelings, feelings that are a leftover of the instincts.

"It's no secret that in the West we don't have the smarts to work with elephants. In the West we lock up the elephant house and then go home. The only time you really think elephant is when you go back again in the morning and turn the key in the elephant house.

"In Asia? It's totally different. In the evening they put their elephants next to the place they live, like you or I park our cars in the carport. They care for that animal twenty-four hours a day. They sit down at the table and they talk elephant. It's a never-ending discussion about elephants. All the time. Day in, day out. They have been talking elephant all this time, for the last three and one-half, four thousand years.

"In the East if an animal does not live up to expectations,

they just turn him loose—toss a few firecrackers after him, let him go back into the jungle.

"In the West man has to conquer the animal."

• • •

Cindy crossed the California border in a truck. Near midnight on December 14, 1982, she arrived. At the Wild Animal Park the doors to her truck trailer were opened. A thirty-four-year-old elephant named Nita walked around it. This gave Cindy a chance to smell another elephant. Because Cindy had trouble backing from the trailer, she was finally harnessed to matriarch Nita, who nudged her. When Cindy emerged into the night air she snuffled her trunk along the ground. Leashed with sixty-five-foot chain, she was led into the barn and put between Nita and the smaller Cookie.

Jeff Jouett went to the park that first morning and watched Cindy from the observation deck. "She reminded me of a big scared kid. She ate dirt. She had never seen it." Several days later Jouett returned. "When the show elephants went by, trunks holding tails parade-style, poor Cindy was so scared she ran to the barn, which by then was a safe spot for her, and hid. Her big rump—two, three tons—was hanging out of the barn. But she believed she would not be seen if she didn't see them."

Zoos are not new. The Chou dynasty in 1100 B.C. kept a zoo, called "Intelligence Park." Ancient Greeks and Romans caged lions, tigers, leopards, bears, elephants, giraffes, camels, rhinos, hippos, ostriches, crocodiles for slaughter in gladiatorial contests, a practice that was halted during the reign of Emperor Theodosius, in the time of that theriophobic Gregory of Nyssa. Renaissance explorers brought back a bounty of animals and "wild men" as trophies. In A.D. 1100 Henry I established a menagerie in Oxfordshire; Henry III moved the menagerie to the London Tower, where it remained until 1828. Montezuma established zoological gardens at Tezuco in the middle of the fifteenth century.

Cortez came upon aviaries and fish ponds at Itztapalapan. The French, helped by Cairo, maintained animal collections over four centuries, only to come close to losing them to hungry nineteenth-century revolutionaries.

The San Diego Zoological Garden exhibits a wild animal collection of five thousand animals, thirteen hundred species. It began with a half-dozen monkeys, coyotes, and bears left over from the Panama-California International Exposition of 1916. The design of the zoo emphasizes natural settings and eschews cages, using deep canyons and isolated mesas to make caging of even large cats and bears unnecessary. But for all that, even *this* zoo of moats, glass, canyons, reminds you of prison.

The lemur, prowling behind glass, swinging, shaking small sticks, the serpents coiled in sand, look like framed collections.

"Lie down, Cindy."

The four-ton Asian elephant goes down on her haunches and rolls over to one side on the concrete pad. She looks like a Mack ten-wheeler turned over on the freeway.

The early morning is hot in the San Pasqual Valley where the San Diego Wild Animal Park's two-and-one-half-acre elephant yard stretches up toward sun-baked hills. Alan Roocroft, the Zoological Society's elephant-training supervisor, plays the hose across Cindy's hide. The dust with which she has sprayed herself sluices off her belly with the running water. Cindy lifts her outside foreleg and paws the air. To an observer, it appears that Cindy enjoys the gentle hosing.

When the bath is done, Roocroft says, "Stand, Cindy." Her giant ears flutter. She rises to her feet. Cindy shakes and water drops fly. The six-foot-long trunk, actually an extra-sensitive nose with forty thousand muscles, lifts and forms an easy loop.

Offering Cindy an apple, Roocroft remarks that she is one of the easiest animals he has trained in his career. Cindy takes the apple with her trunk and deftly places it between her four breadbox-size molars.

"When Cindy is out in the elephant yard, she is an animal with other animals. When she is with me, she is being taught. She knows at my command at any given moment how far she has tolerance. I have bred that into her. That is the basis of teaching."

Roocroft's passion for the massive beasts began in Manchester, England, where he was born. Before Sri Lanka closed its doors to the export of elephants, they were easily obtainable. Roocroft explains, "Our local zoo had a lot of elephants come through." Each elephant was accompanied by a mahout, or keeper/driver, who stayed with that animal until it became acclimated. "These guys stuck to Manchester." His father, a Manchester Zoological Society member, adopted one of these keepers. The keeper took a job at the local zoo, working with the elephants. And at fourteen, Roocroft, eager to begin work with elephants too, left school and took a job digging graves until he was old enough to start at the zoo.

He stayed at Manchester one year. Then he went on to the Chester Zoo, working there until he was twenty-one. The keeper there sent him to Sri Lanka. "Sri Lanka is one hundred seventy miles long, an island that rides off the southern tip of India in the Indian Ocean."

To get to Sri Lanka, Roocroft sold everything he owned. On arrival, his host, a keeper at a zoo in Colombo, gave Roocroft food and shelter.

"What attracted me to Sri Lanka is that there you've got everything you want. You've got the wild elephant in the national parks, you have the worker elephant in the logging camps, and you also have the zoo elephant. So I had three different aspects of the elephant in a day's drive from one another. I got a chance to participate in working with the more docile elephants, but mostly I listened and I watched. It was a real experience seeing people work with animals that *we* call unmanageable."

A change in philosophy followed Roocroft's arrival in San Diego. For years it was said a woman could not achieve dominance in the elephant yard. Roocroft, who insists the ability to work with elephants is not gender-related, has a woman keeper working directly with the animals. There is less talk of "establishing dominance" and more of "making and keeping contact with the animal."

Roocroft sees training as "occupational therapy" for the captive elephant. "They are grateful for the diversion," he says.

By eight o'clock in the morning the five female Asians and four Africans, two of which are babies, are out of the zoo barn. While one of the keepers forks out the first of the day's thousand pounds of hay, the elephants' feet, bigger than dinner plates, tread soundlessly across the dirt yard. Dust clouds rise up around the thick legs. At this time of morning, the zoo is so quiet that a passerby can hear the gurgle of water as it is sucked up into an elephant's trunk. The sun, only now beginning to rise over the edge of the yard, lights the dark hairs that stick up around the elephants' heads, producing halos.

The massive shoulders and huge rumps bulge and roll under the gray hide as the elephants proceed toward the hill at the end of the enclosure. They stand on and around that slope, their features set in what George Orwell called "that preoccupied grandmotherly air." They take up dust with their trunks and toss the dust across their shoulders and backs, thereby protecting their easily irritated skin from too much sun and annoying insects. The tails twitch. The dust scatters in puffs and clouds, and the sunlight catches on silicates in dust motes.

Even in their small zoo yard, the elephants are gorgeous to watch, massing together over mounds of golden hay, and then shuffling apart and tossing hay and dust across their backs. But it is at the Wild Animal Park in the San Pasqual Valley that the elephants appear at their best. There, Cindy keeps to herself. After her seventeen years' exile from other elephants, she is still shy. She remains at the bottom of the pecking order. Given a choice, she prefers the company of Roocroft to elephant. But this morning she reaches out with her trunk and grabs some hay from a smaller elephant's heap.

AROUND

7

AROUND

To go from the sunlight and heat along University Avenue to the cool, dark, throbbing pandemonium inside Palisade Gardens skating rink was like being dropped into another world. Skate wheels thunder. The floor guard's screeching whistle percolates up through the collective roar of hundreds of turning skate wheels, through high-pitched laughter and nonstop music.

Mounted in the ceiling, pink and blue neon stars glimmer across a hundred faces—black, Oriental, Hispanic, and white. Swooping, swirling, wheeling, or just lazily rolling across the floor in duos, as trios, or alone, skaters circle in the conventional counterclockwise direction. Some skate forward and others, three and four together with lightly clasped hands, skate rapidly backward. A lurching toddler grabs his father's hand. He cries out, but his shriek cannot be heard in the din. Grasping the railing, a stiff-legged Vietnamese teenager, not trusting himself to glide, lifts first one foot and then another, working his way, hand over hand, around the rink. Three tall and muscular blacks in their late teens, shoulders hunched, an expression of fierce intensity gripping their faces, blur by along the rink's outermost edges at twenty miles per hour. Between these extremes of skill, groups of three and four junior-high-school girls in pastel jump suits—eyes fixed on their male counterparts—skate decorously on one foot. Older dance skaters, in couples, describe formal patterns across the floor. When the deejay in the balcony switches from Whitney Houston's current hit to the livelier "Meet You in the Ladies Room" by the funk-punk Mary Jane Girls, older couples and novices trek to the safety of the benches that surround the rink. Cheering teenagers and fleet, hard-muscled twenty-year-olds then swarm onto the floor, their features setting into cameos as their speed increases.

A café sits at one side of the rink. By six o'clock skaters are dribbling hotdogs with mustard and dipping french fries in ketchup. They crowd onto benches around the café tables. "Do you remember when the organist sat up there," says a rusty-voiced, red-haired woman, pointing toward the rink's northwest corner, "up over the exit sign, behind glass?" People around the table nod that, yes, they remember and begin to name organists, all dead now or moved far away. The redhead says, "The vibrations from the organ were just altogether different from the records."

"And the rink floors didn't have plastic coating," says a second woman, explaining to the nonskater. "Twenty years ago they sprinkled rosin on the floor so your wheels would grip good. They *powdered* those floors! You went in with brown hair. You came out with white hair—from the rosin."

Wheels were fiber or wood. The new wheels, they complain, grip the floor too tightly. "There's no slip to them," says one. "They don't have the roll," says another.

The streetcar cost a dime and matinee admission to Palisade Gardens was twenty-five cents. Palisade Gardens opened in 1946, the first post–World War II commercial structure completed in San Diego. In the late thirties roller skating moved off the sidewalks into indoor rinks and became a national craze. Around San Diego it meant skating at a little rink on Menlo and University called Betty's, the old South Studio, Morty Zellinoff's Trocadero, Ups and Downs, the Silverado Ballroom upstairs at Euclid and University, the Pacific (renamed Skateland right after the war) at the corner of Front and G streets, and rinks in Ocean Beach, Mission Beach, and the Palace on lower Broadway. Rinks stayed open almost around the clock during World War II. Along with workers from defense factories, sailors and marines skated "swing shift" until three and four in the morning at the Trocadero on University and Marlboro. Skaters put on detachable skates and jitterbugged in the middle of rinks. Each rink had its own gang. After school they met at the rink and skated until suppertime. On Friday nights they went stag, and on Saturdays they took dates. In summer they passed days at the beach and nights at the rink.

Couples skated to "I Had the Craziest Dream," "Ragtime Cowboy Joe," "Rum and Coca-Cola," "Green Eyes," and "Sentimental Journey" swelling down from the Hammond in the rink's loft. They slow danced, skates tip to tip, around the walnut floor. There were whistle chains, trios, grand marches, and a boy-meets-girl atmosphere. The lights were turned down low to play a waltz. There was a lot of romance in roller skating, just like dancing.

After the rink at Mission Beach closed for the night, everyone piled into a car, if there was one, or jumped onto a motorcycle—an old Indian Scout or a Harley—and took off for Sheldon's on old Highway 101 and Balboa and stayed there until one or two o'clock in the morning drinking Cokes and smoking.

The Mission Beach rink at Belmont Park, which sponsored a tough and successful roller hockey team, was tops for a form of backward figure skating called rexing.

Rexing developed in San Diego and Los Angeles rinks in the late thirties. To rex is to skate backward, solo or as a couple. Rexing could be slow or fast. Ardent rexers say, however, that the object of rexing was *speed.* They would scream for the organist to play "Saber Dance" for that reason. Cutting in and out across a rink, one rexer could dominate the floor with this fluid speed skating.

Male rexers used to cut tops off boots to free the ankle for movement. Women would either not lace their boots at all or would run laces through only two or three eyes and wrap the extra shoelace around the instep. Everyone ground down the wooden wheels to reduce their size and increase maneuverability. A rexer recalls: "With the wooden wheels and wooden floors, you could get such speed going you would think you couldn't negotiate the corners. Which is why the rexers always had little wheels—the only way you could get around the corners."

During World War II local rexers in the service carried their detachable, ground-down wooden wheels into skating rinks around America. Rexing San Diegans at out-of-town rinks would either be kicked off the floor for cutting in and out at high speeds, or the rink would be cleared to permit the rexers to demonstrate their skills. No one outside California had seen anything like it.

Rexers were considered tough. Occasionally a group of rexers from the beach would make a raid on the Roller Dome in Hollywood or on a rink in Long Beach. You had to have detachable skates, to get your skates off right away when the fights started.

On Palisade Gardens' opening night in 1946, regulars from every rink in the area showed up to try to dominate the new floor. But no one succeeded. Manager-owner Johnnie Wright was trying to promote a dance-oriented rink. He didn't want it taken over by rexing gangs. But rexers persisted in trying to put their stamp on the North Park rink. By the fifties, the Rebel Rexers, a rexing club whose members wore Confederate army caps, had unfurled a Confederate flag on Palisade Gardens' walls and made the rink their home.

Skaters did the jitterbug and the fleahop wearing skates. After Pearl Harbor, at the Trocadero they raced for war bond stamps. If you won a race, you got a dollar's worth of stamps. There were nights when eight hundred people lined up outside for the Halloween costume party. For Christmas the rink was decorated with tinsel and greenery. For "sweet sixteen" birthday parties mothers brought rosebud-frosted cake for the girls and boys. There were hundred-mile skate-athons for charities, "Live Deejay Broadcast and Roller" parties to which girls in ponytails wore circle skirts embroidered with poodles and crinoline petticoats under the skirts.

"Then television came . . . and everybody stayed home," says Wright. The downtown Palace closed. Then "TV got old, and skating came up again." New rinks were built at Mission Beach, in El Cajon, Chula Vista, Santee, La Mesa. There was even an open-air rink on the Convair parking lot. Some hung in. Others failed. Wright has seen another big drop during the last few years.

Palisade Gardens had rules, says Johnnie Wright. "Until the late fifties, girls wore skirts here. The skirts had to be fingertip length—you stand up, put your hands down, and your skirts could be no shorter than where your fingertips came, which was just above the knee. So if you had real short arms, I guess you could wear shorter skirts." Wright did not permit jeans. "That was a way of keeping out the so-called rougher element. We always felt if a kid had to put on a decent pair of pants, he'd be more likely to behave himself. That was the rule for many years until jeans became the dress."

Until 1958 the music came from the Hammond organ. For the dance skating popular through the fifties, strict tempo was so important that rink organists used a metronome. "A good dance skater can tell you if your music is off two beats a minute," says Wright. During the organ's reign, "Rickety-Rickshaw Man" was the rink's most requested tune. "It was the fastest." Among other popular tunes through the fifties were Tommy Dorsey's "Boogie," "The Breeze and I,"

"String of Pearls," "Moonglow," "Chattanooga Choo Choo," and "Cow Cow Boogie." Wright recalls that "tangos were good, all the marches, the waltzes. For couples, only the organist played a waltz, fox trot, or a hundred-beat boogie." When Elvis Presley emerged in 1956, Wright would not play his records. "We were against that stuff," he says with vehemence. Wright winces. "The kids weren't going for organ music anymore. They wanted rock and roll. But you couldn't get that from an organist." Wright confesses that he did not know what to do at that point and continued to use an organist part-time and recordings of organ music made especially for skating when the organist was not there. Then, in the mid-sixties at a Roller Skating Rink Operators Association meeting, a Texas rink owner told Wright, "I gathered up all my old rink music, dropped it in the river, and bought the Top Forty. Now the only thing that bothers me is going to the bank. The moneybag is too heavy."

"That stuck in my mind," says Wright. "Then one day one of the Girl Scouts came up to me and said, 'Mr. Wright, when are you going to play some music we can understand?' That is when we started gradually changing over."

When disco came along in the mid-seventies, Wright liked it, "It was great for skating" he says. "Just the old swing beat coming around forty years later with a higher tempo." But he has not liked much music that has come along since. Heavy metal and punk rock he calls "impossible."

In 1760 in London an inventor demonstrated the first roller skates. By 1790 skating had become popular all across Europe, but the wheels—made of ivory, wood, or metal—had rollers of all the same size, and *only* forward skating was possible. When an American invented the "rocking skate" in 1863, it became possible for the first time to skate in curves. By the thirties, Wright says, "it was a matter of taking a clamp skate and putting it on a pair of football shoes. We had shoe skates at the Troc before the war, but not many. When we opened here, because of the shortages from the war, we couldn't get shoes. By 1947 or '48, we began to be able to rent shoe skates. In the middle fifties, we stopped using the clamp-on skates. Now anyone who has a pair of those old rink clamp-ons has a collector's item. I sold mine, one skate at a time, for skateboards. Because, of course, we invented the skateboard here in San Diego! So I sold all I could get my hands on."

Fewer than a dozen roller rinks are still open around the county. Now that he is retired and the rink closed, Wright says, "It will take me a while to get used to Saturday nights free, and holidays. When everyone else has been playing, I'd have been working . . . as few as six and as many as twenty-four hours a day. It's been like giving a party."

•   •   •

Flo Sperbeck talks about 1921. She was eleven. Her father, mother, younger brother, and their white collie took the train to California. Already she had lived in Atlantic City, Philadelphia, New Jersey, Scotland, and Canada. California's population was 3.4 million. Sperbeck says, "San Diego was a sleepy little town, very prim and staid. My mother loved it. But we hated it, my brother and father and I."

They lived in a furnished house on the corner of Redbook and Union. Next door a family raised a milk cow and laying hens. ("Can you imagine that? Right there in San Diego! Cows!") The two-story house had four bedrooms, a stable, a tennis court, and bird's-eye maple furniture. The rent was fifty dollars a month. Flo's second-floor bedroom extended onto a balcony with an unobstructed view of San Diego Bay, where she would stand and watch navy ships slice the flat water.

Tom Wilson had brought his family from Canada, where he had gone during World War I to join the Royal Air Force. Very gifted at math, he was to help out his brother, Dr. John Mills Wilson, a dentist, by doing his books. Dr. John had set up a large office at the corner of Third and Broadway and employed nine dentists and a score of assistants. In addition to balancing the ledgers, Tom also drummed up business for his brother, who saw himself as "an advertising dentist." An ambitious practitioner, Dr. John bolted a dental chair to the cab of an old Maxwell truck and went out looking for customers. At the San Diego County Fair, Flo Sperbeck's father demonstrated his superb mathematical skills by doing difficult computations in his head before large crowds. "He draws the crowd," Dr. John liked to joke, "I draw the teeth."

Dr. John would call for volunteers to climb up in the chair, where he would actually pull teeth while the crowd watched with awe. "You see," he would say, congratulating his patient and holding the bloody molar aloft, "dentistry is now painless."

When John opened a second dental office in Los Angeles, Tom Wilson moved the family north. He continued working for his brother, but he also opened a ballyhoo stand to draw dental prospects "for Uncle John by hiring a man to lie shirtless on a bed of nails." In L.A. he eventually realized his true calling when he became a chef at the Biltmore Hotel.

"My parents grew up in a Victorian era. They imposed the same restrictions on me that they had left home and come to this country to get away from. My father, for instance, did not approve of makeup. When I was a senior in high school, he sent me home from a party at my aunt's house to wash my face because he noticed I was wearing powder. I didn't own a lipstick until I was twenty-nine years old."

Peter Drummond was the first Scottish fellow to come courting. "He was the first person my mother trusted me to go out with." She married in 1929, two years after graduating from high school in Los Angeles. She was not, she says, as much in love as she was eager to get out of the house. If a good Scotch-American girl wanted to leave home during the waning years of the Roaring Twenties, marriage was the only respectable way to go. "I would never have disobeyed my parents," Sperbeck says. "I would never have, for instance, just run away."

Flo Wilson, at nineteen, and Pete Drummond were married the year of the Great Crash. For a young couple with few resources, it was the worst of times. By 1935 Flo had had two children and the economic outlook remained bleak. There in Los Angeles, she walked several miles each day with her shopping bag to stand in long lines of hungry people. Her shopping bag would be filled with surplus vegetables—carrots, turnips, potatoes, lettuce—which she carted back to her Highland Park home on foot. The four of them were living on a State Relief Administration budget of forty-eight dollars per month, until she found a job: clerk in the auditing office at Bullock's. Salary: twenty-five cents an hour. "I used to wonder how some of us survived."

Sperbeck and Drummond separated and she took her kids back to Oakland, where her father was working as a chef in several of the Bay Area's better hotels. Flo moved into her parents' home and took a night job at Capwell's department store in the auditing office. Her salary: twenty-five cents an hour. During the day she looked for other work.

"I went to insurance companies, and they said, 'We don't employ married women. Come back when you get your divorce.' I stood in line all day for an application to take the clerical examination for the State of California for a temporary job that paid eighty dollars a month."

Sperbeck took a series of temporary jobs. Times were hard—twenty thousand teachers were out of work in the U.S. College graduates worked alongside her as she went from clerking in a surplus commodities outlet to clerking at the gas company, and then to a clerk's position in the Department of Motor Vehicles. What she wanted to do was to go to college and become a social worker.

"What I regret now, more than anything," Sperbeck says, "is that I never had an education. It's frustrating to be intelligent and not have the education to go with it."

Sperbeck and the children, eleven and eight, had moved into an apartment of their own. She worked eight hours a day, six days a week. Then came 1941, Pearl Harbor, mobilization. Women were being put into what had traditionally been men's jobs. But the growing number of automobiles in the U.S., as much as the war, made possible Sperbeck's first contact with police work as a clerk in the traffic division of the Oakland Police Department. She was thirty-one and scared to death. She had never even been in a police station.

She had wanted to make a good impression and wore her best red suit, a gold blouse in an Indian print of red and green, and a large gold felt hat with red and green feathers bobbing off the brim. To be fingerprinted for the job she had to walk all the way through the men's jail to the fingerprinting office. Prisoners pressed against the bars. "They whistled and they called out and cheered." Her starting salary was 140 dollars a month.

"That traffic divisions office was a mess." Her supervisor, a motorcycle officer who had been injured and put on light duty, "had his own filing system all those years—cigar boxes under the counter. People who received a parking ticket either paid or did *not* pay. Either way, nothing happened. I turned the parking-ticket section of traffic violations from a wastebasket into a paying project."

She decided she would become a policewoman. "Why do you want to do that?" an officer asked. "I've never met a woman in police work who was a lady."

A detective from Sperbeck's department turned to the guy, snarling. "Well, you've met one now," he said.

"That was the kind of reputation policewomen had in those days," Flo explains. "They were floozies: running around in bars, hanging out with the guys, doing a lot of drinking and carousing."

In the spring of 1947, raven-haired, ivory-skinned, and frankly voluptuous, Flo Sperbeck became an officer in the police department of the city of Alameda. "I was sworn in and it was nothing. It was 'Here's the badge. Here's the key to your police box. Here's your whistle. You're a police officer.'" Sperbeck's assignments: work with juvenile offenders and victims; rape and sexual abuse; search, guard, and transport women prisoners.

She proved an exceptionally gifted interrogator, so good at acquiring confessions and the cooperation of suspects that her chief, more than once, asked, "Drummond, do you promise them something?" Her fellow cops started calling her Bulldog.

"I appealed to the better part of people. In sexual abuse cases, I would try to help the accused person realize he needed help." She thinks women, more effectively than men, can question suspects in sexual crimes. "Men allow their anger to show. Male officers get so mad at perpetrators of sex crimes. I was upset, too, about the victims, but it didn't help, if we wanted cooperation in a case, to get angry with the criminal.

"I have always been able to separate the person from what the person does. I could hate what they did without hating them."

The City of Alameda had not had a murder case in forty years. During Sperbeck's seven years there, they had two murders, both committed by females. "The saddest was a young woman who had killed her baby. She put it in her sewing basket and sat on the basket until the baby died. Then she wrapped the corpse in a blanket and put the bundle into the incinerator.

"I sat with her in the prison hospital. She was strapped to the bed. If you came close, she flicked at you with the ends of the straps."

The second case was a woman who shot her husband. "He was running around on her, and one night while he was sleeping, she shot him. She was such a docile little thing. She said to me, politely, 'You want to look in my pockets?'

"Then she asked to call an attorney, Leo Sullivan, a very well known man in his field. I said to her, 'How did you know to call Leo Sullivan?' because she just didn't look like the type who knew those things. And she said, very sweetly, 'Oh, my husband told me if I ever got into any trouble, call.' "

In 1950 Sperbeck turned forty. North Korea attacked South Korea. Her twenty-year-old son, Gordon, was in the navy. Then in July, her daughter, seventeen, died. "She had a congenital cyst that the doctors could not locate," Sperbeck says. "Today they would have found it."

"I became a recluse. I went to work. I came home. I slept. I overate. I kept getting fatter and fatter and less and less interested in what was going on in the world outside. One day, I woke up and realized I had to do something about myself. I went and took a modeling course. Not to become a model but to do something about my lack of self-esteem. I joined Jack LaLanne. I put on my sweatsuit and went religiously, three times a week. And that was when Jack LaLanne had the only school in Oakland. They didn't have machines then. You had to do all the work yourself, with barbells."

She worked for several police departments: Catalina, Contra Costa. Her enthusiasm for life had begun to return. With the postwar baby boom generation beginning to enter adolescence, specialists in juveniles were in demand. But Sperbeck also had become an expert in sex crime investigation and was called in for a good many each month. "Everything from child molestation to indecent exposure."

In 1964 her life changed dramatically. She had met her man, a criminal attorney, and she had fallen in love. And Flo Sperbeck retired. "On the day Ivan and I were married," she says, "October 10, 1964, I wore a pink dress and a little pink hat with a veil on it."

Ivan Sperbeck was a brilliant criminal attorney, extremely handsome, and he dressed "like someone out of *Esquire* magazine.

"We had wonderful years together. We went to England and Scotland. We took a cruise to Mexico. We went to all the Raiders' games." Not content to sit idle, she had acquired a private investigator's license and did much of her husband's investigative work.

Ivan Sperbeck died of a heart attack during the University of California–Stanford game in 1970. "He was simply the most interesting person I ever knew," Sperbeck says. "Each person has a little section of your heart no one else can have." Ivan lay claim to quite a piece of hers. After her husband's death, Sperbeck picked up her life again. She continued as a private eye.

Nobody calls her Bulldog anymore. Most of her clients are defense attorneys for whom she performs pretrial investigations: she locates evidence and witnesses, she interviews clients and witnesses and takes their statements. She is the oldest woman in California working as a private investigator. With twenty-three years of law enforcement work to her credit, and twenty years as a licensed private eye, Sperbeck is the grande dame of the profession.

Some days Flo Sperbeck pulls on a stringy white wig and a pair of faded jeans. Seventy-three years old, her hair is paper-white now. She wriggles into her stained fishing coat and deliberately buttons it up wrong. She takes her worn shopping bag from the closet and goes out on assignment for an afternoon of undercover sleuthing.

Her assignment is to visit each outlet of a Bay Area chain of stores behaving like an elderly woman who has had too much to drink. The stores' clerks and security guards are being advised by her boss on how to spot methods of shoplifting. She is to steal what she can without being caught. Sperbeck fills her shopping bag with blouses, jewelry, nylon stockings, underwear. She takes a pair of slacks from the counter, rolls them up and shoves them inside the fishing coat.

At the next meeting of store managers, Flo Sperbeck appears with her hair back in a bouffant upsweep and wearing a navy blue dress. She walks to the front of the room and dumps out her heisted loot on the table. Each item is tagged. She calls out the store from which the slacks came, and then the jewelry, and on through the heap of stolen merchandise. The managers parade to the table to pick up their articles.

Flo teases the hair high off her forehead into a froth of soft curls. Her skin is still ivory smooth. "What keeps you from the bad memories," she says, "are the good ones."

CHILL OUT

8

CHILL
OUT

Working with corpses, he says, doesn't bother him; he's grown up around it. But it has never become routine.

"If it gets that common to you, you should leave it. Any family that gives me the privilege of treating their dead I treat it as if it was my own relative. I respect the body. In the mortuary I put my own laws on. The body is never left nude. The reproductive organs are always covered. I don't allow joking around, no carelessness, no dropping of the body. I know they can't feel it, but I don't want it that way."

Hartwell Ragsdale, Sr., is a big man, over six feet and two hundred pounds, stocky, coffee-colored, with short crinkly hair. He has on a light gray suit, a vest, and a pale blue silk tie, polka-dotted with white. The pin of a fraternal order is tacked to the tie.

Since Hartwell Ragsdale opened his mortuary in 1956, he has prepared an average of three hundred San Diegans for burial each year: eighty-four hundred in total, almost all of them black.

Racism has fostered and protected the black funeral industry. In the late thirties, Swedish scholar Gunnar Myrdal was hired by the Carnegie Corporation to research black life in America. He discovered that black barbers, hairdressers, and undertakers were alone among black Americans in having exclusively black clientele. White people simply did not wish to touch or be touched by the black. "Negro corpses," Myrdal reported, "are segregated even more meticulously than live people."

Prior to the 1964 federal Civil Rights Act, only two San Diego mortuaries and two cemeteries would accept blacks. The two cemeteries, privately owned Greenwood and city-owned Mt. Hope, set aside areas alongside the railroad tracks running through the properties and reserved them for Negroes. That changed. Today no mortuary or cemetery in San Diego County will refuse a body. In fact, Hartwell Ragsdale says, "Most mortuary businesses are able to survive by picking up this minority business, which in the past they did not want." The change has come partly from new laws but also as a result of cremation's effect on the funeral business. "One-third of all mortuary business is direct cremation, cremation without prior embalming, and the profit is small." Hence minorities have become attractive to the funeral industry. "Blacks, the Spanish-speaking population, Asians, Filipinos, Samoans don't go for direct cremation." Only fifteen percent of Ragsdale's customers even ask the cost of it and only four percent choose it.

White-owned mortuaries now bury black and other minority groups' bodies, and some have hired minority employees. Ragsdale is called by few white families. "We bury perhaps one white person a month."

After a funeral, Ragsdale makes at least one home call. If he feels concerned about a family, he may go back a second, even a third or fourth time. "You go by, you see how they're doing," he says. This is one of the many aspects of a family business that Ragsdale says he learned from his father. "And my father," he points out, "learned it from his father." It is a theme he iterates again and again—that the funeral business in the black community is a family business, that he learned, almost absorbed, from his father.

Ragsdale's grandfather and father used a hand pump to embalm. The electric pump, which Ragsdale rates as faster and cleaner, was not available until the late 1930s. "Like any change, it was resisted," Ragsdale says. "My father wanted one, but they cost two hundred dollars, and it was either buy a pump or a car, and he bought a car. It was 1940 before he bought his first electric pump."

Ragsdale cannot recall the first time he saw a body. Both his father and grandfather were undertakers, as are his brother, uncles, and cousins. He and his brother, Lincoln Ragsdale, and his parents, lived in the other half of his father's Ardmore, Oklahoma, mortuary, while Ragsdale was growing up. (When he moved to San Diego, his own two children grew up in the second-story apartment above the Imperial Avenue mortuary that was his original place of business.)

He does remember that when he was sixteen, he got quite a scare the first time he went alone to pick up a body. "A fellow and his wife had separated. He had come up to her door and knocked, and when she answered, he blew part of her face off and then he went off in the weeds and shot himself.

"The police were there when I arrived. It was summer and the Johnson grass had gotten up pretty high. You couldn't see the man. The police told me to go out in the grass and pick him up. I was as scared as I could be. I crawled up on the man. He was in a sitting position in the grass. He had taken his shoe off and, with the shotgun under his chin, he had put his little toe into the trigger. When I got right up on him, his eyes were wide open and I thought he was looking right at me. I got up and ran."

His grandfather, William Ragsdale, was born in Magnolia, Arkansas, in 1849. In the late 1890s his wife's brother, a U.S. Marshal, was living in the Indian Territory. "In those days it was under federal law, and run mostly by the Indians," Ragsdale says. "They had freedom there for black people, and my grandfather's brother-in-law told him to come over into that area. There were more opportunities for black people . . . and at least the law there was a little different. They didn't have so many lynchings and hangings."

In 1896 Ragsdale's grandfather opened a livery stable in Muskogee. "It was like a modern-day taxicab service." After the grandfather had been in business for several years, renting and leasing buggies and horses, he noted he received frequent requests for wagons to pick up coffins. "He decided he would start building coffins in the back of the stable." The pine coffins were body-shaped, large at the shoulders and small at the feet. Soon he was renting buggies on one side of the building and furnishing undertaking services from the other. "There was no embalming in those days. A person was buried immediately and the funeral might not be until six months later.

"People didn't have time during harvest or when the crops were going in." The elder Ragsdale would go to the home, help relatives wash, dress, and lay out the body. Both blacks and whites bought his coffins, but only blacks hired him to help prepare the body.

Until the Civil War, embalming was a rarity. Bodies were buried or kept on blocks of ice, or in tanks of formaldehyde. But during the Civil War, when men from the North died in the South, and vice versa, families wanted their dead returned home. Dr. Thomas Holmes, father of American embalming, was the first person to preserve bodies on a mass scale. Holmes went to the front and embalmed bodies en masse, billing each of the families of the fallen one hundred dollars. He prepared 4,028 bodies and returned to Brooklyn a wealthy man, a millionaire in today's dollars.

In the early years of this century, a Dr. Reynard came to Oklahoma to teach Grandfather Ragsdale to embalm. Reynard was traveling the Southwest, Hartwell Ragsdale says, "instructing people on how to embalm. He would stay with you for three weeks. If you didn't get a person's body to embalm within three weeks, he would extend the period up to the time you got somebody. He would show the individual how to embalm and in exchange he would get to sell you the instruments and supply your embalming fluid. The fluid was shipped by rail in fifty-gallon wood tubs. Once my grandfather was able to embalm, he could hold bodies over for two or three weeks up to the time of a funeral service. This would give people time to gather relatives."

Grandfather Ragsdale trained his seven sons as undertakers. But Muskogee, Oklahoma, was small, so each son went to another town, settled, and opened his own funeral home. Things weren't always calm. "There had been race riots in Tulsa in 1921," Ragsdale says. "Racial things were not good in Oklahoma at that time." One son, back from service with the U.S. Army in World War I, was killed by the Klan, his body dumped behind his father's Muskogee mortuary. He was on his way to pick up his wife from her job as a schoolteacher. The men who killed him had confused him with an escaped convict.

In 1930 Ragsdale's father moved to Ardmore, Oklahoma, to open his own mortuary. Ragsdale's mother, an elementary-school teacher, had graduated from all-black Langston College in Oklahoma, and continued to teach and to help out with the business. She was particularly eloquent and did much of the mortuary's publicity and visiting of bereaved families. Occasionally she would organize picnics out in the country for fifty people at one time, and would use the opportunity of the gathering to talk about funerals and the necessity of preparing oneself for death. At these picnics she would sell burial insurance.

One son, Lincoln Ragsdale, was a pilot in World War II. He served in a segregated unit stationed near Phoenix, where he quickly discovered that Arizona had not one licensed black funeral director. So in 1948 his father purchased property in Phoenix for Lincoln and Hartwell and they acquired a loan to open a new funeral home. In the wintertime, Hartwell recalls, "I'd feel beautiful." But when the weather in Phoenix turned hot, he felt sick. Eventually he learned that he was allergic to air blowing across water stagnating in evaporative coolers, the precursors to modern air conditioners, used in Arizona in the mid-fifties. But by then he had already moved to California where he "*always* felt beautiful.*"*

Ed Anderson, who had owned the mortuary at Twenty-sixth Street and Imperial Avenue, Ragsdale says, "had just passed. So I did some surveys and never found one person in San Diego who said Mr. Anderson had been unfair. As he had no children and no relatives, I decided when I bought the mortuary from his estate, I'd keep his name on it." The Anderson-Ragsdale Mortuary's first year in San Diego was financially tenuous, but after that, he says, "I had become acquainted and my business began to improve."

Ragsdale watched San Diego grow. Before World War II, he says, the black population in San Diego County was small, three or four thousand. "There was no industry, nothing then to draw black people here. There were three blacks on the police force, four in the fire department, and two in the city school system. Once the Reverend George Walker Smith got on the school board, he changed that! Our present police chief began to open opportunities for minorities. Because of affirmative action many departments in the county and city began to open up to blacks. Now we have a black population of fifty-five thousand in the city and eighty thousand in the county, with a black middle-class population of about five thousand."

As the black community grew and became more permanent, more people chose to be buried in San Diego. "It used to be that bodies were shipped back home," Ragsdale says. "There would be a service here for friends and family and then a second one at the home burial place. But only ten percent of the people do that now." Once members of the black community followed a southern way of "celebrating a home-going." A wake or series of wakes were held before the final funeral service. These were in the home. The body would be displayed in an open casket in the living room. Food was brought and shared, and for those who wanted it, Ragsdale says, "whiskey was always there . . . but it was outside, usually in the yard. There would be barbecue," he says, smiling. "The wake might extend over three or four nights, depending on a man's station in life, his age, on how many lodges and organizations he belonged to. He might have served under three or four pastors, and each of them would preach. The preacher who pastored him forty years before, he'd lead the service the first night, and then the next man the following night, and so on. They'd end up the last night at the church with his present pastor. Then the next day the funeral services would be held." There are few week-long wakes now.

The undertaker is white America's most mistrusted businessman. Yet the black undertaker, together with the black schoolteacher and minister, has traditionally been looked up to, even admired, in his community. The place of the funeral and his role in his community are at such variance with the practice and attitudes of the white majority that when Jessica Mitford wrote her funeral industry exposé, *The American Way of Death,* she decided not to include black mortuaries. "It would have been an entirely different book," she said.

"For a black person," says Hartwell Ragsdale, "calling the mortuary is not like calling the plumber or the electrician. Families want to see a person they know. They expect to shake your hand, to hug and kiss.

"I'll go to the cemeteries and off in the distance I'll see a funeral for white persons. There will be two or three cars, seven or eight people. That would *never* happen to a black person. If he has any connections with anything, there will be fifty people at the graveside, and that's small."

In the Southeast community, in a few short hours, people will know that someone has died. In families, as soon as word comes that someone has "passed over," cousins, sisters and brothers, aunts, grandparents, and even in-laws will gather. Ragsdale often holds a body for five or six hours to allow a family time to come together. Friends will visit the family, go by the funeral home to a wake there on the night before the funeral, and everyone will take off work, if necessary, to attend the graveside services.

Death is often the only event that brings a fragmented black family together. It is as much a reunion as a mourning together. Afterward there is always a big feast to joyously celebrate the home-going of the deceased. Even among the more educated this tradition has hung on: the funeral service, almost always an occasion of communal jubilation rising out of personal grief, with hymns, buoyantly sung, triumphantly shouted, and loud.

In the black middle-class churches, emotionalism is discouraged. There the service follows the standard order of worship—calm and subdued. In more Pentecostally inclined Protestant churches, men and women clap, sway, trace out with their feet a "blues shuffle." Individual voices build a complex harmony of hymns and gospel tunes, inviting in the Spirit to move among them. Such a service may culminate in a frenzied Pentecostal prairie fire, with participants speaking in tongues, praising, testifying, remembering the deceased aloud, even speaking out about their own future deaths.

Hartwell Ragsdale explains, "We believe in paying respect to our dead. Our philosophical and religious belief is that you go to heaven when you die. A funeral service is a farewell party to our friend or family member. It is an important part of our end of life, and it is very rare that we don't have a crowd. As often as once a month we will have a funeral with a thousand people there. Death has always been an important part of black life . . . not birth."

There are two colleges of mortuary science in California, one in San Francisco, from which Ragsdale graduated in 1948, and another in the Orange County community of Cypress, from which his son, Hartwell III (known as

"Skipper"), graduated last year. Both offer two-year courses in funeral services: classes in anatomy, physiology, chemistry, and restoration. But it takes longer than two years' study, Ragsdale stresses, to become truly skilled at restoration. "I can make a person look like they did in health," Ragsdale says, "building the tissues back up, getting the color back in. And I know it helps families; it helps them to accept that death has occurred. And if six months later a family still has not faced that fact, you have not done your job."

Ragsdale began embalming when he was sixteen, and he explains the process (for which he charges 150 dollars) in a manner as straightforward as that a librarian will use to tell you how to check out a book. The body is washed and its orifices sprayed with disinfectant. An incision is made in a vein to empty the body of blood. (The blood goes directly into a holding tank to be disinfected, then into the sewer system.) An arterial incision is made to fill the body with embalming fluid, replacing, ounce for ounce, the body fluids that have been removed. This solution contains formaldehyde, glycerin, borax, phenol, and alcohol, and dissolves in tap water. Colorants and emollients can be added to restore skin color and to improve skin texture.

"Embalming-fluid manufacturers have become very scientific, very technical. Now each company has its secrets and its various brands." Ragsdale laughs. "Just like Rinso and Duz."

After transfusion is complete, aspiration begins. A trocar, a hollow needle to which a tube is attached, is used to puncture the abdominal and chest cavities. Fluids are removed from and replaced in these areas, the removal and replacement done with an electric pump.

Ragsdale takes great care in the final dressing of the corpse, even to a detail as small as perhaps tucking a lace hankie into folded hands.

Ragsdale is weary. One of the last San Diego mortuary owners who does his own embalming (only thirty-eight percent nationwide still do), he was up late the night before, preparing the body of a man who turned a gun on himself.

"We had two suicides recently. One gentleman had been out of work and the other had woman trouble."

The latest suicide victim was in such bad shape that Ragsdale advised the family not to show the body. But he knew they wanted to open the casket for viewing. "Anybody that dies, somebody cares," Ragsdale says, explaining that he worked through the night to reconstruct the shattered features of the man's face. Wincing, he adds, "I had to build him a new nose."

His mortuary offers what may be the least expensive funeral, with embalming, of any San Diego mortuary, but he is careful to make sure that a family can afford the funeral it chooses, if for no other reason than that he needs to be paid.

"Encouraging families to overspend is bad business as well as bad ethics." It is bad business because the mortuary is left with an unpaid debt on its services rendered and a residue of ill will in the family one has to dun to pay its bill. In some cases, he will "throw in something free" rather than have a family accrue a larger debt than they can pay. If another family member should die and the Anderson-Ragsdale Mortuary bill is still reading past due, the family will most likely seek out another mortuary. The black mortuary business is built on the individual, Ragsdale says. "I have to live in a way so as not to bring shame or scandal on the name. I don't want anyone to be able to say to my son, 'Your daddy was a scandal. He got me to overspend.'"

Ragsdale's business continues to show a healthy five-percent-per-year increase. The mortuary handles an average of three hundred bodies per year. Ragsdale admits he could make it financially with two hundred bodies, "but only because it is a family business." That helps keep down the overhead that includes buying new hearses every two years and keeping the mortuary staffed around the clock, 365 days of the year. He hopes to pass the business to his son, an inheritance increasingly rare in the industry. "Most mortuaries in the area, the average person does not even know who owns them now," he says. Only four local funeral homes are still owner-operated, and the rest are run by large corporations. Until the last decade the funeral business remained a family operation. Fathers passed it to sons. Inflation, recession, unemployment, a nationwide shift from embalming to cremation have all hurt the funeral business. Now many smaller mortuaries have been swallowed up by corporations that cut their costs by streamlining operations. An aggregate of mortuaries can be administered as one multiunit mortuary, with centralized bookkeeping, transportation, embalming, and cremation.

Ragsdale's brother, Lincoln, solved his mortuary's financial problems by changing the name of his Arizona business from Ragsdale Mortuary to Universal Memorial Center and actively going after white business. He took down his pictures of Martin Luther King, Jr., and Booker T. Washington and "put up some white folk." He hired white personnel. By 1977 his business had increased more than three hundred percent. "For every black body I get," Lincoln Ragsdale told *Black Enterprise,* "I have three white ones."

When he was a child, Ragsdale remembers how afraid he was of death and dying, despite its familiarity in his life. "All the time I was growing up, my prayer was every night, 'Don't let my father and mother die until I can take care of myself.' Now I know that was kind of selfish. But you see, I knew that death was the only thing that could stop them from taking care of me."

Ragsdale's parents died long after he had moved to San Diego. Their deaths hurt. "But it was their time," Ragsdale says, "and because my father said he wanted to be close to us, they are buried here."

Death had never deeply upset him until 1977. "The only time death really stretches you is when it happens in your own family. My daughter was killed in a one-car accident up by Oceanside, coming back from mortuary college. She was nineteen years old at the time.

"Death affected us more deeply than many families I deal with. Being a funeral director, I was supposed to be conditioned to death. And I . . . but only on the surface. Underneath I went through some horrible torment. I thought

God had been unfair to me, and I would ask myself, 'How could God have treated me so mean?' But I have looked at it for a long time now. I think there was a purpose in it. I know now what the feelings are of parents when a son or daughter has passed. I help better.

"For so long I was afraid of death. But the death among our loved ones has changed that. I realize I have to die. I am not afraid of death anymore. I have now, you see, as many friends and relatives outside of this life as I have inside it. I used to be afraid of what happens after death; I don't like what I don't know in the future. Now I am not afraid even of that. Enough people I was in love with have passed, and if there's anything to this, I will be joining them. If they went anyplace, I want to go with them."

TINSEL AND SAWDUST

9

TINSEL
AND
SAWDUST

When I was a child I went to the circus every spring. I looked forward to it. I also dreaded it. I was scared that a tightrope walker would plunge down onto the ground and explode like an overripe plum. I was terrified that a trapeze artist would miss her catch on the swing and sail into a far wall where her head would smash like a cherry bomb, or that a tiger would chew up a trainer—suit and entrails and hair—like I had seen an owl in a film chew up a mouse. Before the circus and afterward, my dreams would fill up with brightly colored images, like those in my comic books.

As I walked onto the grounds of the Circus Vargas, all that came back: the excitement, the longing and the fear. I recalled what had frightened and thrilled me as a young girl.

Faster-than-the-eye spins, long teeth, and sharp fangs. Mascaraed eyes. Open claws.

You remember bare skin. The women hang upside down, streaming their long hair like romantic fairy-tale princesses. They pull upward and reach across empty space, even as they hang by an arm, an ankle. Biceps, triceps, deltoids—every muscle bunches, ripples, knots, flattens. Spotlights wash the pale limbs paler and intensify the scarlets, violets, aquas. Spangle-encrusted fabrics sparkle. The eyes are exaggerated. The smiles, too. I could see why, at ten, I had awakened from dreams of the circus, sweating and terrified, and why at the actual performances I would often feel dizzy and sick to my stomach.

"It's older than Jesus," Congo said, meaning the circus. Congo was sloshing a gray string mop up and down in a bucket of sudsy pine-scented disinfectant. Putting down the mop, he leaned against WOMEN, lettered in gold paint on one side of the red eighteen-seat rolling outhouse built onto a sixteen-wheeler. He drove the vehicle. He cleaned it and slept in a space above its cab.

Circus Vargas had set up that morning. Men had been pounding steel sledgehammers on tent stakes since sunup. People dressed for office work, mothers and a few fathers pushing strollers and holding toddlers' hands, and whole classes of schoolchildren stood watching the usually vacant lot on which the circus was rising. A few people were buying tickets for the night's performance. Behind the chicken-wire fence were thirteen elephants, seven llamas, two camels, and thirty horses and ponies. Next to the larger animals under a canopy was a children's petting zoo, with geese, ducks, guinea hens, sheep, lambs, goats, and one black yak.

Camels munched hay. Behind them, hobbled at the legs with hunks of logging chain, stood one long row of elephants. The elephants' big bones seemed to move under skins that were no more than shrouds of ashen fog. They lifted hay with their trunks and tossed the long stems back onto their shoulders. A hatchet-faced man in blue jeans and canvas work gloves passed a hose to each elephant, one after another, along the line. Each elephant offered the hose grabbed it with its trunk, then turned the nozzle into its mouth, clamped down on it and drank. A roustabout, bare to the waist, pushed a hay-filled red wheelbarrow between the lines of llamas and elephants. Sweat funneled down the hollow of his spine and ran in lines down his tanned sides.

Meanwhile at the far end of the elephant row, the ten-thousand-pound male elephant extended his penis. The penis was two feet long, pink, and spotted with black splotches. The elephant lifted his trunk and trumpeted, then threw his trunk across his neighbor's head, letting it rest there. With terrific pressure, he spewed urine onto the duff. The urine made a depression in the ground.

"Looka dat elephant pee!" a boy said, one of two dozen first-graders lined up along the fence. KENNETH was lettered on masking tape stuck to the back of his jacket. The elephants bumped shoulders. The kids—Kenneth, Takeda, Val Shoudou, Jabari, Kahil, Earth, Al, and Mitzi—also bumped shoulders.

Congo had finished cleaning the toilets. "Those kids, they always comes around," he said, wiping his hands across the belly of his Circus Vargas T-shirt. The shirt had shrunk. A quarter-moon of Congo's heavy brown naked stomach fell over his belt. He sat down on the steps that led up into the truck's toilet stalls, patted the rubber treading, and said, "You set here with me, girl." I did. He said, "I seen you 'round this morning, watching the animals. I never know whether to talk to womens. They can get the wrong idea." He pointed up to where he lived in the truck's cab. "I got the world's smallest TV in there, 'bout this big." He used his hands to make a square the size of a cracker box. "I watch all them soap operas. An' I read a lot." I asked what he read. "I read about presidents." He said his favorite presidents were Harry Truman, "from the Show-Me State," and Roosevelt. "Because they did something for the common man." Low in his throat he said, "I'm the black sheep of my family." He scratched at his graying grizzled black beard, looked across at me, and smiled.

I asked how he liked working the circus. "I like it fine. It's like ever'thing. All the world's a pretty picture 'til you walk in. Circus ain' no different. Out in front a picture looks good, don't it girl?" I nodded agreement. "An' the world's the same—pretty. In front. There's sadness in the world. Down inside it. I got my own sadness. But it's not here." He pointed toward the red-and-blue Big Top. On all four fifty-six-foot center poles American flags blustered in the breeze.

"Folks gets happy here. They can forget they's whole families livin' in cars and eatin' out of garbage. You know that, don' you?" He looked at me, hard. "Do you want to know why I see what's behind things? Say yes if you do." I said yes.

"I travel. I was in World War II in the Philippines and Puerto Rico. Then I was on Union Pacific. I was Brotherhood of Sleeping Car Porters. I made up the beds, brought their coffee, slid the menu under their doors, an' waited for 'em to write what kinda eggs they want. I heard 'em cry out at night, too. Sometimes they'd come out and say, 'I can't sleep, Robert.' Robert, that was my name then. An' I'd say, 'You go take yourself a walk in the lounge car and drink a big cup a' black coffee, then you sleep.' I done this circus now for eleven years. Every town I come to, I walk. An' I look aroun' and see I got something' better here than what most folks have. But I got my own sadness like ever'body. This morning I sat down over there by the water an' I just let my tears go. Ever'body's got it. You got it, But you jus' gotta get it out."

He asked if I would like him to make me a cotton candy. I said, "No, thank you," and he said, "You an' I got in common that our mamas taught us good manners." He asked if I were going to go to the circus. I said I was. He said, "This is a real good show this year. Goes past so fast you think it's been a dream."

Congo is correct. The circus is older than Jesus. The Romans, twenty-five hundred years ago, screamed through chariot races in the Circus Maximus, whooping while half-naked men battled hungry beasts. When a Roman satirist said, *panem et circenes*—"bread and circuses"—he meant that all most people want out of life is food and entertainment.

I asked Congo if he knew the nuns who traveled with the show. Sister Priscilla? He nodded.

"She leaves me peanut-butter-and-jelly sandwiches and an apple up there in my truck. I gave her a plant last year for Easter. She's still got it hanging in their window."

I followed his directions to their trailer and introduced myself to Sisters Lorelei, Joel, and Priscilla.

The sisters all work in the wardrobe truck and as concessionaires. They eat and sleep, work, study, and pray together in their one-room house trailer. Next door is the tiny chapel housed in a Chevy 310 van. On a clothesline strung between it and their trailer hang their blue chambray smocks.

The Little Sisters of Jesus live in groups of three or four. They do manual labor to support themselves and live among nomads and migrants. These three have chosen the circus people as their mission.

"Contemplatives in the midst of the world," says Sister Joel, smiling broadly. "Rolling hotdogs into buns all day is an activity that encourages contemplation."

Of the three, Sister Priscilla was the most familiar with the life they committed themselves to. Tanned and slight, with dark eyes and dark graying hair pulled behind her chambray scarf, she speaks in accented English. Her father's family, she explains, are Swiss and have been circus people for five generations.

They told me the tale of their order's founder, Charles Eugene de Foucauld, born into an aristocratic French family in 1858, orphaned, then trained at St. Cyr for the French Army. He kept a mistress, partied, gambled, and before he turned twenty-five had thrown away his fortune. In 1883, guided by a rabbi, he explored Morocco. Three years later, he reconverted to his Catholic faith. By 1890 he had become a Trappist monk, but by 1897 he had left the Trappists. In 1901 he became a priest and went to live alone in the Sahara. He hoped to attract other Europeans to his desert mission, but drew none. He wanted to found a new order. No one came. He hoped to win converts among the Islamic tribesmen, and failed. In 1916 Foucauld—by then known as Brother Charles of Jesus, the Universal Little Brother—wearing a patchwork heart and cross sewn to his robes, was shot by a soldier from a warring desert tribe. Twenty-three years later a woman inspired by Foucauld's writings opened an order of nuns.

"It's a rough life, especially for the roustabouts. These men don't have family," Sister Joel explained. "They are often completely out of contact with their parents and sisters and brothers. They come and go from one show to another."

• • •

The Duraskin polyester tent keeps out light. Even on a sunny afternoon, it is dark inside the tent. Twelve spotlights are set on platforms twenty feet up. The spots focus on the action in each of the three rings. The beams cross the dark tent and flit up spangled legs and down sparkling backs.

Ringmaster Joe Pon's whistle shrilled across the tent. The lights came up. Pon strutted across the ringmaster's platform, lifting his aqua top hat high. The audience of five thousand cheered. He crooned through his hand-held mike, "La-dies and gentlemen, boys and girls," his voice a candied basso, "astonishing, brilliant, magical, mystifying . . ." He announced David Pol: "His temperamental, tempestuous tigers transcend terrestrial three-ring tradition!"

Sixteen Bengal tigers came slinking into the center ring. Spotlights struck the black transverse stripes rippling across their tawny pelts. The tigers spat and prowled, and gave off a heady pong. Pol ordered his tigers to sail through flaming hoops. He snapped his black whip and the tigers leapt atop their stands. Pol commanded poses and the tigers assumed prim Victorian postures, ears at attention. The audience ooh'ed, then aah'ed.

A ten-year-old girl in the front row held her nose. "I always hold my nose at tigers," she said. Her blond hair had been rolled into Shirley Temple curls. She pressed the popcorn box between her knees and rested her hands, covered with dimestore rhinestone rings, in the lap of her flowered skirt. A dark-haired Latina in the next chair kept saying to her, "I think I'm gonna' be sick, Sabrina," and Sabrina answered, "Not me. I'm havin' too much fun."

The tigers raced through a steel chute winding out of the ring, and through the tent opening, into the circus backyard. Uniformed men pushed brooms around the center ring. Clowns filled up the three rings—white faces painted with frowns or smiles, their hair orange and green and purple, with poufs around necks and wrists, stomachs poked-out and hands rubber and outsized, striped pajamas and polka-dotted suits, red rubber noses and ears, three-foot-long saddle oxfords. One clown inserted a funnel into the other's waistband and poured water into the opening. The audience hooted, waiting for the water to spill out, and aah'ed when it didn't.

"La-dies and gentlemen, boys and girls. The astonishing aerial ballet of nine brave and beautiful aerial artists daringly disregarding danger . . . *the Web!*"

Nine women strutted out, three for each of the three rings. Spotlights glittered red off their bikinis. Each paused before a rope and kicked off her high heels. Like monkeys, the spinners climbed thirty feet up the ropes. Once they had reached the top, the nine tuxedoed attendants below grabbed a rope and took up their positions. The men whipped the ropes, the women spun, faster and faster. Sweat slid off their muscled backs and legs and arms and their madeup faces.

The dark-haired child let go her popcorn box and squeezed Sabrina's wrist. "I'm scared."

"Not me," Sabrina said, and shook off the hand.

The temperature inside the tent went into the nineties. The yeasty smell of the audience blended with popcorn oil, hotdog spices, and tiger musk. Thirty feet in the air, where on a hot day the temperature can reach 130 degrees, the women turned, twirled, twisted, then hung upside-down by their ankles.

Relief cut through the audience as the nine spinners shinnied back to earth. Clapping did not stop until Pon announced the chimps and bears. Suited, hatted, and shod, the chimps sat quietly in straight-backed chairs while the bears, wearing hats and shirtfronts, pedaled unicycles. The audience relaxed. Then Pon introduced "Les Victoria— living statues from France," giving *France* a naughty nasal vowel.

Benny Williams rode out standing astride his elephant, Anna May. He wore a leopard-skin bikini and a leopard-skin armband. A leopard-skin headband held back his shoulder-length blond hair. Over his shoulder he carried petite Lynn Pope, looking helpless and lissome in her leopard-skin-and-gold-lame bikini and leopard-skin armband. Her long hair cascaded down over Benny's bare chest. Atop Anna May, the duo paraded to the center ring. Benny lifted Lynn high above his head. She lay back on his upraised palms as if floating.

A handler led in Benny's leopard, Nirvanah. Nirvanah pawed the sawdust. Nirvanah growled. Lynn stood, legs apart, on the elephant's back. Nirvanah jumped to the elephant's shoulders. Lynn knelt, pursed her lips, crooned to Nirvanah, petted her, rubbed her, cooed, and called to her: "Nice kitty."

Benny stood downring, chest out, admiring Lynn, his elephant and leopard. He extended his arms and coaxed the spotted cat down. Nirvanah hesitated, rubbed her muzzle against Lynn. Benny urged the leopard forward with his hands. Nirvanah leapt off Anna May and landed with her forepaws on Benny's bare and hairy chest. The audience shrieked.

At the finale, the elephant curled her trunk around Lynn's tiny waist and then slid her past the sawed-off tusks and took her ankle into the pink, salivating mouth. Lynn dangled upside-down, hair drooping toward the sawdust while Anna May galloped the circumference of the ring, running faster with each round. The crowd, awed and quiet, could hear the elephant's feet thud against the concrete.

Congo is correct when he says the show goes by like a dream. It is suggestive and tantalizing phantasmagoria. Spins, long teeth and sharp fangs. Claws. Twinkling sparkles and spangles. Bare human skin. All apparently meaningless and yet just about to converge on some triumphant meaning.

Each performance ends with the Grand Parade in which the entire roster of performers makes a farewell circuit of the football-field-size tent. Caparisoned elephants, blond-maned horses, white-faced clowns, aerialists, jugglers, fire-eaters, magicians—all waving good-bye to the cheering audience.

Then, dripping sweat, the performers exit, stripping off their spangle-encrusted costumes as they go. They head straight out of the tent into their vehicles, already hooked up and ready to go.

●   ●   ●

While bleachers are packed up, rigging taken down, and the gigantic tent struck, the circus acts push on. By eleven o'clock that night they are well along their route. Every few miles "confidence arrows"—sheets of bright paper with black arrows—lead the circus caravan toward the next site. An arrow pointing downward means slow down, one to the right means sharp turn approaching.

At the next circus grounds a white cross etched in the asphalt marks the spot the center pole will rise. East of it will be the midway, main street for the public. To the south will sit the cookhouse, and west from it a double file of performers' quarters begins to take shape. They are "smashing in." By 3 A.M. the village is nearly complete. Poodles, miniature schnauzers, Pekingese, and terriers hop out of pickup cabs and motor homes. Tails wagging, they sniff out one another. Bright light from trailer windows scatters on the ground.

"This is their home," says Mike Gorman, the advance man responsible for the logistics. "They are regular households and this is their evening."

—135—

The miles traveled may be ten or two hundred. The drive may take an hour or all night. "When I'm in my truck and driving, I always feel really happy," said Lynn Pope, trapeze artist and partner of Benny Williams. "I think I like just the process of going places." On arrival, "even if it's the middle of the night, or almost, the first thing you look for is a coin-op laundry and a grocery store."

During a typical week the circus's three hundred animals, its star performers, its technical assistants, maintenance and concession staff perform sixteen separate times and move the entire show twice. Forty-six weeks after opening day Circus Vargas will have traveled over twenty thousand miles and performed eight hundred times.

Circus Vargas is twelve years old. It is one of the three largest tented circuses left in North America. After Ringling's began to perform only in buildings, the tented circus went on the decline. But now, circus aficionados say, it is coming back. Two other tented circuses—Carson and Barnes and Cole Brothers—Clyde Beatty—remain.

It takes more than a hundred vehicles—campers, house trailers, vans, pickup trucks—to move the circus. Two full-sized diesel flatbeds carry the seventeen-ton Big Top in ten canvas-wrapped bags. Four semis haul the four giant center poles, one hundred thirty-six support poles, and five hundred stakes (made from car axles) that secure the poles to ropes. Another semi moves the two Clark 125 Bobcat forklifts and a Rube Goldberg stake-pounder with which three workers can pound the four-foot stakes into almost any surface. Other trucks haul electric generators, spotlights, bleachers, fences, folding chairs, concession stands, ice-cream wagons, the ticket wagon, and the Bubble Bounce trampoline.

Before Circus Vargas pulls into a city, the marketing staff has been in place for three to six weeks. It has rented an office, hired posterers, and handed out half-price coupons for children's tickets. Doug Goodrum, a soft-spoken Tennessean, managed the circus's three-day stand. He handed out over one million coupons to local merchants. Goodrum obtained licenses and permits, arranged radio and television promotion, publicity, and advertising, placed help-wanted ads for thirty temporary workers, and ordered the three thousand pounds of oat hay and four hundred pounds of sweet feed that the thirteen elephants eat every day. He found freezer space for enough meat to feed sixteen Bengal tigers—meat that is sent air freight to each of the circus stops.

Goodrum had also put in orders for delivery of special feeds for the brown and black bears, the fifty or sixty horses and ponies, seven llamas, and two camels, for the thirty Samoyeds in Circus Vargas's Canine College, and the two lions, Benny Williams's leopard, Semon's chimps, for the pigs, goats, ducks, guinea hens, geese, the yak and long-horned sheep in the petting zoo. Not to mention hotdogs, buns, soft drinks, ice, syrups for snow cones, popcorn for the concessionaires, propane and butane, sawdust, toilet paper, gravel. He had also gotten the mail from the Lakewood, California, home office, and handed it over to Sister Priscilla to sort. The advance promoter has ordered the sawdust, dumpsters, septic service for the portable toilets, located the local horseshoer, vet, hospitals, and contacted the paramedics who will be on hand, in case.

In natural light, close up and out of the three rings, you have trouble connecting the performers with the costumed daredevils who swing, climb, ride, hang by ankles, suspend 180-pound men from their teeth. The performers look shorter, slighter—ordinary.

The silver knee-high boots showed wear, creases and scuffs. They had black marks and were ground down at the heel. Jugglers' royal-blue tight-fitting trousers were washworn polyester with the same nubbins, pile and pulls along the fabric one sees on any matron's stretch pants. Sequins were coming loose. Seams had ripped. Dried sweat left white half-moon salt stains on dark jackets and tunics.

Lynn Pope was born in Waukegan, Illinois. She got a BFA in theater and film from the University of Wisconsin. She trained as a gymnast, a dancer, a mime, and a clown. Her background is typical of that of many women in the larger touring circuses, in Ringling's Red and Blue units, the Cole Brothers—Clyde Beatty Circus, in Carson and Barnes' Circus. She had not planned on a circus career.

"It just happened. I'd wanted to be a dancer. But at five-foot-three I'm too short. After college I got involved in the Festival of Fools in Europe. Then I came to San Francisco and worked with Make-A-Circus. After that I worked for three years as a Ringling showgirl. During that time I decided, 'I can do more than be a showgirl.' I put together a trapeze act."

Pope auditioned the act for Ringling's. "Satin," the first black female aerialists ever to perform in Ringling's, won out. "I auditioned for Circus Vargas, was hired, and came on. I left my boyfriend at Ringling's."

Pope tutors two children from one of the circus families. Vanessa Thomas, one of the nine web-spinners, with a master's degree from Temple University, also tutors two children.

"The Circus Vargas kids," Thomas explained, "use mostly Calvert Correspondence School materials. Every course comes in a complete package, with workbooks, a teacher's guide, the textbooks, right down to the last little pencil and pad of paper." Although third-, fourth-, even fifth-generation circus families still tour through Europe and North and South America, Pope said, "the circus family is deteriorating." More and more children leave circus homes, go to college, and choose settled professions.

Circus Vargas currently boasts several second- and third-generation families nonetheless. One is the family of fifty-five-year-old Rex Williams, the Boss Elephant Man. Rex Williams leaned over the fence separating animals from visitors. Chewing a long blade of oat hay—"the best damned hay in the world"—Williams rolled up the sleeves of his blue-and-gray plaid shirt, pushed his cowboy hat back on his head, and pointed to the hills. Williams's thick neck is furrowed, sunburned, and leathery, and the hand he put out to point looked as tough and as scarred as the elephants that stood behind him, rummaging with their trunks. "You know, I been with the circus forty-two years. I ran off from home in the northeast hills of Arkansas when I was thirteen, and I've been movin' ever since. I look at those hills off there and they are so green and so pretty it kinda' makes me want to stay."

Williams's thirty-two-year-old son, Benny, performs essentially the same Tarzan-and-Jane elephant-and-leopard act that Benny's mother and *her* father (who ran away and joined a circus when he was fourteen) first routined. In Benny's teens he replaced his grandfather in the act. A few years ago, when Benny's mother "retired from the bikini," Benny "put the loincloth back on and re-routined the act. But it is still essentially the same thing my mother and grandfather were doing when I was a kid."

Benny Williams lives in a furniture van he has converted into an on-the-road home for himself, Anna May, and Nirvanah. When I asked if the van didn't smell pretty high on hot days, Benny said, "Sure! It's a cozy smell. It means I'm working."

Rex Williams, his second wife, Eva, their fourteen- and nineteen-year-old daughters, Renee and Darlene, and Benny perform together. Rex and Eva present and train the elephants and horses. Their daughters ride the horses. Benny changes out of his loincloth into a tuxedo and puts the llamas through a circle dance.

Head showgirl Dione Paray is a graduate of the University of Arizona. Those who fail to differentiate between circus and carnival annoy her. "People who don't know anything about the circus think of us as 'carnies,' as drifters. Circus performers, generally, are just not *like* that." Paray stresses that a strong sense of community, much like that in small-town middle America, binds circus performers together.

"Even when we move on to another circus," Paray said, "we stay in touch and we keep track of each other." Paray's trailer home certainly supports the contention. It is just like any modest small-town home. Only her costumes and headdresses, laid out on the couch for the afternoon's performance, belied the comparison.

"Circus is a hard life," Vanessa Thomas said. "It's very hard work. We have to take awfully good care of ourselves." The women eat carefully and sparingly. Until the last show of the day is over, the spinners and aerialists eat very little. "Hanging upside-down with too much food in your stomach," Paray says, "does not work."

The female performers meet in the tent after the last show, put a Jane Fonda workout tape on the VCR, and do an hour of stretching and aerobics. The effects of aerial work show in the women's muscular shoulders, backs, and arms. "The dancing takes care of your legs," Thomas said, adding, "We weigh in quite heavy and far more than we appear to. It's because we are mostly muscle.

"Most of us are pretty humdrum people," she said. "We don't do anything particularly wild in our personal lives. When you have to get up in the morning like I do and face eleven Samoyeds barking for their food, you don't do anything crazy the night before." Thomas, like many of the Circus Vargas women, performs several times in each show. She takes one rope on the web spin. Later she puts her set of Samoyeds through their Canine College act. Wearing a fifteen-pound rainbow headdress, she rides an elephant in the finale.

They watch a lot of television. They shop for groceries. They cook and bake. Write letters. Work out. But some of the tent and maintenance crew, the prop men and animal keepers, appeared to lead more chaotic lives. Many do not stay long. There is drinking and drug use among the crew members. I had stood outside the Big Top's back door and seen two tough-looking prop men open beers during an afternoon show's intermission. One of the executive staff walked up and spoke harshly to the drinkers. "You can do that on your own time," he said. "Get rid of it. Now!" The men grumbled and swore, but they poured the beer onto the ground.

In all but two or three trailers, shades are pulled down. For the roustabouts, last night was the first night's sleep since the last stand. Snores rasp from the two dormitory trucks even while the odor of coffee wafts from the cookhouse. The chalkboard menu offers navy bean soup, eggs, hamburgers. Outside six folding chairs and a picnic table have been set up. The men have a ten-dollar-a-day allowance.

I sat on a plastic-wrapped bale of hay with a sloe-eyed tent crewman. He bought me a Coke, eschewing one for himself. "I've given up sugar," he said, laughing as he lit up two inches of cigar stub with a kitchen match. A smoke-cloud rose above his off-center face. His yellowed teeth had grown unevenly, the way kernels on an ear of corn grow during a drought. "One day in my twenties I just gave it up and went," he said. "I was in a café eating my fried eggs and I said to myself, 'Do I wanna nine-to-five today? Hell, no.' I been on this circus two years now. I'm a copout. This isn't the real world. No phone bills, no utilities, no house payment, no wife or children. But I never much liked the real world when I was in it. Sure it's rough. But I keep myself up. I been takin' Shaklee vitamins for six months. And I sleep good. Not ever'body can say that."

I asked about the men who work with him. "About half, mebbe, *were* somethin' and the other half's been drifters all their life—people that can't settle down. It beats the gutter." Asked if there was much socializing between performers and crew, he scuffed his round-toed boot in dust and straw. "Naw, they're friendly. But they stay to themselves." I asked if he met women and took them out. He did. "Mostly the townies that come around. I met one here last year and we had a dinner and a nice dinner wine. It keeps you civilized. Gets out your bottle of Christmas aftershave."

What did he imagine himself doing in twenty years. "I'm thirty-four now. Before that I hope I get movin' out of my blood. Hope I'll stick someplace. Mebbe raise a family. I put money by." Was the pay good? "Like ever'place else," he said and shot spit straight out from the gap between his front teeth. "I got brothers and sisters, all married and divorced and remarried. Kids all split up. So it ain't so good for them. But sure, I'm human. I get lonesome. I wish't I had a place. What gets me is in the supermarket I see a woman puttin' a big roast in the cart."

We watched the elephants, the camels and llamas. "See, over there?" He pointed toward the tentsite. Two men, stripped to the waist and sweating, brought fifteen-pound sledgehammers down on tent stakes. "See how he can't keep that hammer going smooth? Look at the next guy. He's got that smooth easy action. He just brings that hammer back and around, back and around. You can tell temporaries from the regulars by how they handle that hammer. These bucks they hire on get worn out fast. They think it's gonna be great, that they'll join the circus, and after an hour they just start waitin' to be back to where home is."

Terry, another roustabout, shares with four others the back end of the trailer truck that carries the circus sound studio. "The circus makes use of every space," says Terry, "just as if it were a sailing ship." His life, he says, is not all that different from that of the itinerants of his native England who carted their trained bears through market and cathedral towns during the Middle Ages.

Unlike performers and staff, roustabouts have no contracts. "They could fire me today, or I could leave today. There are no firm strings." Most of the men, he says, "are young guys, itinerants, wanderers. You don't get many, anymore, of the typical kid, run-away-to-join-the-circus types. Oh, you get one or two. They want the glamour of associating with circus people. They will practice juggling with them in the Big Top, but they have no firm ambitions to be performers."

In his fifties, an Oxford graduate in sciences and economic history, Terry left his wife, children, his job in an English ad agency, home in the English countryside, and came to the States. "I had not liked Americans in Europe, but I came here to California and adored it."

A fat white duck, penned at the back of a camper, pecks corn, oblivious of the llama trotting past. Clotheslines hang between the trailers. A new rock hit drifts out of several doors, mixing with shouted orders, the growl of engines and the pinging of fifteen-pound sledgehammers driving stakes.

SELF-HELP

10

SELF-HELP

Judith Wilson is a dwarf. She wears children's sandals, a girl's size-twelve sweater. In her shoes, she measures four feet in height. When she was two, her family physician diagnosed her irregular growth as achondroplasia, an improper development of the bone cartilage that causes congenital dwarfism, epitomized by profoundly short legs and arms, blocky hands and feet, and a normal-size head and trunk. Married for almost twenty-five years to six-foot, two-inch Gary Wilson, Judith is the mother of a five-foot, ten-inch daughter.

She met Gary Wilson when she was twenty-seven. "I used to think, 'Oh, well, maybe one of these days.' Mother would tell me, 'The right person always comes into your life when the time is right.' And then Gary appeared!" He proposed and they were married in Japan, where he was stationed with the navy.

She knows other small people who are married to average-size individuals. Many small people become parents. "A lot of them have the 'little littles,' as we call little people born to little people, as well as average-size babies."

When she became pregnant, she weighed seventy-five pounds. The last months of the pregnancy she spent in the hospital, in bed, fed intravenously. At birth, baby Julie weighed six pounds, nine ounces, and was eighteen inches long.

"The doctors didn't know where I put her. They said my inside was the size of an eight-year-old child's."

Her daughter had difficulties when she first went to school. "The children used to say to her, 'Your mother is a midget. Your mother is a dwarf.' They were very cruel. She used to come home devastated, and then she went through a period when she became hostile. She would say to her dad, 'Why didn't you marry a taller lady?'

"It used to upset me, but I thought, 'Now, what am I going to do about this?' Something had to be done. I spoke to the principal at the school and said, 'I think the best way for me to deal with this situation is to be at school. The more I'm around the children, the more they get to know me, the better off it will be. Then they won't think I'm an oddity, that Julie's mother is a freak or a witch, as they think I am.' So I volunteered to tutor, and I worked at the library, and it wasn't very long, a couple of months, that children would come up and say, 'Oh, you're Julie's mom,' and a good rapport developed. Her friends eventually thought the world of me. We had children over here all the time. They'd be in the kitchen, on my stool. They thought it was wonderful that they could reach. They'd even do my dishes!"

The logistical problems are myriad being so short. Life goes on several feet overhead. Your eyes graze adults at thigh and belly level. To talk with parents, teachers, and even older children requires tipping your head back. The sink rim hits you chin level; on chairs your legs dangle or stick straight out. Stairs must be negotiated one at a time; dropping a coin into a street pay phone is impossible. Supermarket shelves might as well be Everest.

All the furnishings and appliances in her house are of normal proportions. While she would someday like to have everything customized to her height and size, it is difficult if you have average-size people in your family. "And if you want to sell a place, it becomes a problem," she says.

"The most aggravating thing for me is to go to the bank and want to write a check. The counters are so high I can't reach them. I can't get to the Ready Teller machines unless I have a stool."

Finding clothes, particularly dressy garments, is nearly impossible. She and a dressmaker shop together. When Judith Wilson sees something she likes, the dressmaker sketches it and makes it for her. High heels have to be specially made. There are physiological problems as well.

The diamonds Judith Wilson loves glitter on stubby fingers. "So small and chubby," she says, explaining that her hands lack strength. She cannot sew, for instance, because cutting with scissors is too strenuous. Pushing a vacuum cleaner across the floor wearies her quickly.

"A big saucepan of potatoes—to try to lift the pan, hold it, drain off the water—that's a difficulty. Gardening is a bear. I hate gardening. I loathe it. It's like doing penance."

People stare. "I don't let that bother me," she says. "You become used to it. The time it's really noticeable is if a child stares and says something. Then, often, the mother feels embarrassed, and she either spanks the child or herself will make rude or loud remarks. That brings it more to my attention than if she simply let the child look at me.

"You have to think you are good and wonderful. You have to build that barrier around yourself, so that you don't allow yourself to be hurt."

In Egyptian, Greek, Roman, and pre-Colombian cultures, dwarfs were esteemed for their mystical powers. Rulers and courtiers collected them, employing them as jesters, acrobats, and protectors of jewels and precious objects. In 1710 Czar Peter the Great assembled seventy midgets for the wedding of a court favorite; famous artists used them as subjects in their masterworks. Until the nineteenth century, the undersize human being was classified as a *mirabilis hominum,* a human marvel. By the end of the nineteenth century he had been reclassified as *mirabilis monsterum,* or monstrous marvel. The dwarf lost the mystical, mythical aspects of his identity. The discovery that dwarfism is caused by purely natural factors made him a "physical defective." In Germany, for example, troupes of performing dwarfs were popular, but in the Third Reich they were sent, along with Jews, homosexuals, and gypsies, to extermination camps. Recently, in Australia, dwarf-tossing has been sponsored as entertainment by pubs. A Chicago bar tried to organize a similar event.

Some years back Judith Wilson, her husband, and their twenty-year-old daughter were wading in a river, she with her skirt hiked up.

"A little boy," recalls Judith, "about four, came up to me. He was just looking at me, staring, and the next thing I knew, he pulled down my dress, he was so worried about my legs showing. Then he said, 'You are *so* small. Don't you want to grow?'

"I said, 'Oh, yes. I would *love* to grow.' He told me, 'Well . . . do you like cereal?' And I said, 'Yes, I love cereal.' He said, 'Well, I tell you what I want you to do. I want you to go home and eat three big bowls of cereal. Then you go to bed, go to sleep. . . . You'll wake up and you'll be big!'

" 'It *will* work,' he said. 'If you say it will, and you believe that it will.'

" 'I believe it will,' I said."

THE OLD MAN AND THE C

11

THE
OLD
MAN
AND
THE
C

"It was a wonderful home to go to," a student of his recalls. "Something magic about that home—the smells of his cigar, little ones during the day, big ones at night. At one end of the study—a long room—there was a wall-length window looking out onto the garden. Odors from the garden would come through the open windows, and the books themselves gave off the smell of leather." Much of this library had been brought with him from Germany. "There was as much literature as philosophy—all these beautiful old books, the whole house was full of books . . ."

Philosophy books filled the living-room shelves; in the hallway, leading into the bedrooms, was literature—Goethe, Thomas Mann, Sophocles, Euripides. The living room was arranged in such a way that when people sat in it they would be facing one another. There were small couches with coffee tables in front of them, and on either end of the coffee tables, individual chairs. There was no way you could be in that house without being drawn into conversation. People felt immediately comfortable about walking into the kitchen and helping out with a meal.

The kitchen walls were covered with pictures of animals that he had torn out of magazines. At the end of the book-lined hallway, in the master bedroom, shelves and windowsills, dresser tops and pillows were covered with stuffed toy animals friends constantly brought him as gifts.

He lived with extreme modesty. He drank run-of-the-mill wines except for an occasional bottle of something special. Meals in his home were good but not extravagant. His wife drove an old Peugeot. And had to drag him to the store to purchase clothing.

He met his classes, read incessantly, walked daily on the beach, visited the zoo. He loved the zoo. During summers and academic breaks he traveled abroad, speaking, lecturing. By all appearances he was a rather typical transplanted German academic: formally polite and, by North American standards, almost diffident. He did not call students and peers by their first name, nor were acquaintances invited to address him informally. He was Professor Marcuse, never Herbert.

Herbert Marcuse, born in Berlin of upper-middle-class Jewish parents in 1898, had served in World War I. He was a student of philosophers Edmund Husserl and Martin Heidegger in Freiburg, where he received his Ph.D. in 1922, and he was an early master of the Institute for Social Research, more popularly called the Frankfurt School, a group of left-wing intellectuals who hoped to take philosophical speculation out of the academy and put it to work solving practical problems of everyday life. Leaving Germany after Hitler's rise to power, Marcuse came to the U.S. in 1932, settling temporarily in Los Angeles with a group of émigrés that included Bertolt Brecht and Thomas Mann. In 1940 he became a U.S. citizen, and during World War II served as a political analyst in the Office of Strategic Services, the forerunner of the CIA. Afterward he manned the Central European Division desk at the State Department. From 1951 to 1954 he held positions at Harvard and Columbia University, then returned to full-time academic life at Brandeis University in Waltham, Massachusetts.

At Columbia, at the height of the McCarthy period, he had been challenged—pressed to say if he was a Marxist. He said, "Yes. What did you wish to ask me?" Yet he resisted easy classification. In 1958, his book, *Soviet Marxism,* deplored the brutality of Marxism developed under Stalin.

Marcuse taught at Brandeis for twelve years. During the sixties, he gradually emerged as a government critic, speaking out against the Vietnam War and racism. In *One-Dimensional Man* appeared his biting critique of affluent postindustrial society. In it he warned, "Liberty can be made into a powerful instrument of domination."

"Free election of masters does not abolish the masters of the slaves."

The worker Karl Marx had expected to be the agent of revolution was, in Marcuse's analysis, so fat on consumer goods, so lulled by comfort and contentment, that he had become part of the problem, rather than a means to its solution. Only excluded peoples—students, artists, Third World, and racial minorities—had revolutionary potential.

Marcuse was not pro-Soviet, or ever a member of the Communist Party. He was a severe, pessimistic critic and a romantic utopian theorist who envisioned the possibility of a better, freer world, a paradise without cops or management experts and bureaucracies, or hungry children or war. *Pravda* denounced him as one of the "werewolves" attempting to "decommunize Marxism."

Bill Leiss, a graduate student then, describes Brandeis as a "very uptight" institution during the sixties. Marcuse's increasing outspokenness displeased the university's administration. When he turned sixty-five and reached retirement age, the school was willing to offer him only an annually renewable one-year contract.

Leiss, twenty years old and the recipient of one of the first Woodrow Wilson fellowships for graduate study, overheard a casual aside one day and was charmed by the professor who made the comment. Leiss's adviser's desk was next to Marcuse's at registration. Someone mentioned a course on "The Latin Fathers of the Church." Marcuse leaned across his desk and said, "What about the Mothers of the Church?" Signing up for a class, Bill Leiss found the professor's style and intellectual excitement irresistible.

Outside of the lecture halls, Marcuse associated only loosely with his students. "Only in my fourth year at Brandeis did I get my first invitation to his house," says Leiss. Marcuse's second wife, Inge (widow of Marcuse's associate in the Frankfurt School, Franz Neumann), was exceptionally warm and intelligent, and conversation was "rapid fire, intellectual." She and Marcuse were particularly skilled at giving parties. There would be dinners for graduate students and faculty, and dinners for larger groups when an intellectual luminary visited. To go there, for Leiss, was like "entering a shrine."

Erica Sherover was another student at Brandeis who gravitated to Professor Marcuse. She had entered college at sixteen, graduated from Oberlin, and yearned for a break before starting graduate school as a Woodrow Wilson fellow. "What I wanted to do, basically, was to hitchhike around the world and see if I could make my living as a folksinger. I did some of that and then worked at a kibbutz for two years." Counselors urged her to try Brandeis, where she enrolled in the History of Ideas program. Her first contact with Marcuse was in his class in Hegel.

There were two kinds of students in the Hegel class: "Those of us who were the younger and irrepressible ones, who didn't even realize he was a great man—capital *G* capital *M,* and then there were five or six white men students, whom [Marcuse] always referred to as 'the graybeards,' who were very proper, who wore ties and sat up close and basically repeated his own words to him whenever he asked a question. He would say, 'No, no, no! I know what I say, I want to hear what *you* say.' "

Sherover went to Mississippi in the summer of 1963—"to be one of the outside agitators," she says, laughing—and was arrested. When she returned to Brandeis in 1964, she signed up for Marcuse's "Political Theory from the French Revolution to John Stuart Mill." It clarified much of what she had participated in. She wrote a seventy-page paper, applying her own experiences and insights to the question of forging a free society from one that is unfree. Studying with Marcuse, she decided, was the most exciting thing she could do.

In December, Marcuse's *One-Dimensional Man* appeared, winning national and then worldwide notice. From three thousand miles away came an invitation to a symposium sponsored by the fledgling, year-old philosophy department of the University of California at San Diego. The topic: "Marxism Today." Herbert Marcuse was one of four speakers invited by the department's total faculty, all three of them. Instead of a modest turnout, hundreds attended and a furor ensued in conservative San Diego.

With Brandeis having declined to extend his tenure past mandatory retirement, Herbert Marcuse accepted an invitation to teach in UCSD's new philosophy department. Woodrow Wilson fellows Bill Leiss and Erica ("Ricky") Sherover followed him there to continue their studies, as would a brilliant young woman who had audited his courses during her senior year, Angela Davis. So did another Woodrow Wilson fellow, a thirty-one-year-old veteran who was just graduating from Northwestern University, Ron Perrin. He had picked up a copy of *One-Dimensional Man* ("It showed me how philosophy could become practical in a social, instead of only a personal, way") and tossed aside his applications to other graduate schools. John Burke, too, heard that Marcuse would be offering courses in political and social philosophy and relocated from Riverside, California.

Perrin thought the campus and academic situation a "Shangri-la." Classes were small, and with few undergraduates enrolled, the graduate students "had the faculty pretty much to ourselves." However, he felt intimidated by many of the other graduate students. "They were brilliant little brats, all younger than I was and incredibly more erudite."

Coming from the East, Bill Leiss was shocked by Southern California students—"barefoot, carrying surfboards." Ricky Sherover, too. She thought UCSD "quite incomprehensible." "First of all there were all these sort of long-haired students that I thought were hippies. But they weren't. They were surfers. And, it was the only college I had ever been in where male students came to class wearing a bathing suit and nothing on top. I was quite startled."

Bill Leiss thought it an especially "curious place." "Founded around science departments and dominated by eminent scientists, tied into the military establishment through research contracts. And here was this philosophy department which deliberately went out and recruited Marcuse. They brought him in deliberately. They created a situation in which, of all things, the philosophy department became the center of radicalism." At least eight graduate students, "activists with good academic records," came specifically to study with Marcuse.

Meanwhile, during the summer of '65, Students for a Democratic Society (SDS) at Ann Arbor, Michigan, adopted *One-Dimensional Man* as the main text for their teach-ins.

The undergraduates at UCSD were amazingly unsophisticated and untutored. Bill Leiss and Ricky Sherover were Marcuse's teaching assistants for an undergraduate humanities course titled "The Present Age," part of a two-year program. The undergraduate course, which attracted two hundred to three hundred students, met twice weekly for lectures by Marcuse, and once a week in small discussion "sections" with a teaching assistant. Sherover wrote a list of names of contemporary thinkers on the board and asked students to identify each. One was Max Weber. "What I got back was that Weber was the owner and founder of Weber's Bread."

To this undergraduate group were added "some

maverick graduate students—and nothing in between. The mixture was explosive."

Marcuse lectured from sketchy notes, striding back and forth as he talked. Questions—participation—were encouraged, even in the large undergraduate sections. Questioning was at the heart of the Frankfurt School's "critical theory." Students were urged to reflect critically upon their experience and to employ the dialectic or "power of negative thinking," to expose contradictions in commonly held assumptions.

No matter what the subject or course level, Marcuse used primary sources rather than collections of philosophical works that offer abbreviated readings from various authors. He never assigned his own books, and shrank from seeking influence for his own ideas. He never even referred to his own work, and he did not recruit disciples. In a seminar on Hegel, several class members discovered on their own that he had written a book on Hegel's ontology and regarded as a great triumph the evening they were able to get Marcuse to concede that perhaps some class members would benefit from reading *Reason and Revolution,* Marcuse's study of Hegel's revolutionary aspect.

When one came to know Marcuse, says Leiss, "there was never any doubt what his ideological inclination was. But one would not learn this in class." Marcuse scrupulously avoided venting his personal politics in the classroom. With students who approached him outside the classroom and asked for advice and opinion, he was frank as to the nature of his beliefs. Nor did he ever discuss his personal life or history in class. At Brandeis, and later at UCSD, says Bill Leiss, "Students close to Marcuse found it difficult to acquire information about his earlier social or political life."

Even in more intimate settings, Marcuse rarely spoke of himself. It was not that he had anything to hide but that he would have considered it improper to discuss his personal history or problems with students. Perrin: "We never once heard him discuss the political movement in this country within the context of what it meant to him personally. He always spoke of what it meant to him in a historical sense."

Only once, bowing to great pressure from students, did Marcuse offer a course on Marx. Leiss: "Anything I learned about Marx I had to learn on my own. Marcuse simply never mentioned Marx."

Nor did Marcuse encourage his graduate students to write theses or dissertations on Marx. According to Ron Perrin, Marcuse never said "You can't write on Marx" in so many words (and Ricky Sherover in her dissertation did take up Marx). "He would say, 'Write on Scheler, write on Husserl, do the Fichte stuff.'" Perrin believes that Marcuse was acting protectively toward them, that Marcuse feared writing about Marx would keep students from being able to get jobs.

He was charismatic without being flamboyant, and he could be very witty. When his undergraduate course in the History of Ideas and Theories of Society, with several hundred students, was assigned an underground hall in the Humanities Library, Marcuse pointed out the irony that while the cars on the rooftop parking lot were in the sunshine, the students were underground in the dark.

Graduate seminars, held in the evening, lasted three hours. During those hours the class would often cover no more than five pages of Hegel or Kant's *Critique of Pure Reason.* "The outside world," says Leiss, "would be shut out." A student would present a report on the section of text under consideration. Class discussion would follow. In the seminars on Kant or Hegel, Marcuse would always have the original German texts at his elbow. Generally, his students would use the English translations. These were difficult materials, and Marcuse insisted students learn to analyze them, to look carefully at their arguments, and at the implications of seemingly unimportant comments. A seminar group might spend an entire semester on one hundred pages of Hegel or Kant. Perrin: "He situated them in an encyclopedic context." Ricky Sherover echoes this, saying Marcuse insisted upon "a very careful, a *very careful* reading of what the text said, and what it implied."

"Maybe in Europe," says Leiss, "this still goes on. But where in North America could you have gotten a better education?"

Marcuse was a tough grader and particularly demanding of advanced students. He wrote very little on students' papers, and would make what Sherover calls "squiggles, and checks, which meant, 'This is interesting,' or 'This is not interesting.' " Rarely would he write lengthy comments on a paper.

Many students found him unapproachable. Says Leiss, "When you overcame your reluctance and approached Marcuse, you received a warm reception. Students needing help got as much time as they asked for."

While most professors who have graduate students working under them will use their influence to help these students, Marcuse insisted that his students make it on their own. He would not use his contacts to help them find work after graduation. However, when requests came for letters of recommendation, Marcuse never failed to respond, and for those students whose work had been good, says Leiss, "he wrote very flattering letters."

"We were a remarkable group of students," says Perrin. "We were able to complete a very rigorous curriculum, work on our magazine *Alternatives,* organize demonstrations, and pass our comprehensive exams." These lasted an entire week, and, to pass, one had to exhibit familiarity with the entire body of philosophical work. "Everyone knew only half of the people who took the exams would pass." Just as Marcuse's students had done at Brandeis, the group organized, each student taking a specific area, preparing a paper on that area, then exchanged papers and grilled one another relentlessly. Said Perrin, "We did this, in great depth, while we did all this other stuff. The other little bourgeois brats were all preparing individually." To the surprise of everyone, including many of the faculty, all of the radical group passed.

In October 1965 during the first of the International Days of Protest, Vietnam Day rallies were held in a hundred cities around the world. Graduate students at UCSD organized one of the school's first political protests. Although only a small group showed up, Marcuse addressed it. A person who took protest seriously as a political act, Marcuse never talked about its being immature or a stage through which young people were going, or as a youth rebellion. In Marcuse protesting students found someone who believed in them.

During that fall SIL (Students of the Independent Left) was organized and Leiss elected president. Functioning as its "senior-statesman type" or "front man," Leiss became responsible for relations with the administration. "We really were the Marcuse organization in the sense that we deliberately intended to be nondogmatic," says Leiss, and to distinguish ourselves from SDS and "all the other crazy leftists." It intended to be active, but wanted its action to be aboveboard and open. With a membership of roughly one hundred, mostly graduate students from the philosophy and literature departments, SIL was known for its literature table in Revelle Plaza and the magazine *Alternatives,* of which six issues were published. The group also leafleted outside the Selective Service office in downtown San Diego. Says Burke: "People thought that students advising prospective military people of what was going on in Vietnam was treasonous, and we were often harassed." By the fall of 1967, to celebrate the fiftieth anniversary of the Bolshevik revolution, SIL flew the National Liberation Front flag from one corner of their Revelle Plaza literature table. U.S. Navy pilots from Miramar, flying out over the ocean, spotted the flag and alerted the chancellor. The group was identified as students of Marcuse.

Nineteen sixty-eight was tumultuous. On January 30, North Vietnam mounted coordinated attacks on South

Vietnam, the Tet Offensive. In March, peace candidate Eugene McCarthy made a strong showing in the presidential primary and Robert Kennedy, four days later, announced his candidacy. On the last day of March, President Johnson halted the bombing of Vietnam, offered Hanoi negotiations, and announced he would not run for a second term. Four days later Martin Luther King, Jr., was assassinated. Seventeen days later, during student uprisings in Berlin, Rudi ("Red Rudi") Dutschke, West German SDS leader, was shot in the head. Armed Black Panthers petitioned the State Assembly in Sacramento.

In late April students at Columbia University in New York captured the administration building. On May Day militant leftist students, some carrying banners that read MAO, MARX, ET MARCUSE! clashed with police. On June 6 Robert Kennedy was assassinated. In August the USSR invaded Czechoslovakia, and in Chicago, riots and police brutality scandalized the Democratic convention.

On the day King was shot Perrin remembers that Marcuse walked into his class of 250 students and, in European fashion, said, " 'Stand up,' and of course, there were all these San Diego kids, and when Marcuse said stand up, they stood up." While they stood respectfully, Marcuse talked passionately about a society that lives with violence. Seventeen days later the same thing happened when Rudi Dutschke was shot.

After Martin Luther King's assassination TNC (Thursday Night Committee) formed. Far larger than either SIL or the SDS chapter, TNC sought to raise community awareness of racism. Going house to house in San Diego, TNC members discovered few people willing to discuss the issue. Many of these San Diegans, says Burke, interpreted the students' action as "interference and affront." It was rare, he says, that people were sympathetic or supportive.

San Francisco had had its summer of love. The University of California at Berkeley had become a battleground. A significant portion of the U.S. population turned toward the right, including the state's new governor, Ronald Reagan, who had electioneered on the promise that he would clear radicals out of the state universities.

Marcuse was far less active in civil-rights and antiwar movements than such men of his approximate age as pediatrician Benjamin Spock and two-time Nobel Prize winner Linus Pauling. Unlike Marcuse, these gentlemen, indefatigable marchers, were highly visible in newspapers and on television nightly news. Yet controversy swirled around him as student leaders around the world were citing Marcuse's concepts and the media dubbed him "the Father of the New Left" and "Angel of the Apocalypse." "The Marx of the children of the new bourgeoisie," said one periodical.

An Italian television network had sent a crew to San Diego to do a story on Marcuse. TV cameras were set up in the small auditorium in which Marcuse lectured. They hovered over him at lunch with cameras. Then, during the lecture, the filmmakers ran up and down in front of him. "He never missed a beat," says Perrin.

Marcuse made clear he objected to the juxtaposition of his name with those of Che Guevara, Régis Debray, Rudi Dutschke. These were men who risked themselves physically, while he, Marcuse, described himself as "participating in this battle only through my words and my ideas." As to his fame, Burke says, "He resented and regretted that he was a media figure. And he loathed the guru thing . . ."

During the early summer Governor Reagan sent letters to trustees and regents of all the state's colleges and universities deploring the "climate of violence."

"A sick campus community in California in many ways is responsible for a sick community around those campuses."

In mid-May Marcuse and his wife were in Germany and France. Marcuse had been invited to speak. While in Berlin, they visited the gravely wounded Dutschke in his hospital room and soon after the *Bonn Advertiser* quoted an unnamed source as saying Dutschke, with his American-born wife and their young son, had been invited to San Diego to attend the university and work as a teaching assistant.

On June 11, 1968, the *San Diego Union's* lead editorial was headed "This is an Order!" It demanded an immediate investigation of UCSD philosophy professor and avowed Marxist Herbert Marcuse, "professor of Left Wing philosophy." The editorial touched off a furor. San Diegans were publicly outraged at Marxist Marcuse being paid with taxpayers' American dollars.

Marcuse hotly denied the article that had suggested he had invited the German radical to teach at UCSD. But the outcry would not abate. *The New York Times* and *Newsweek* carried the Bonn story. "There were lots and lots of threats," says Ricky Sherover. "He kept a whole mail pouch of insulting and vicious letters."

In July Marcuse received a letter giving him "seventy-two hours to live." It was signed *Ku Klux Klan.* Ricky Sherover insisted that Marcuse take the letter seriously. She wanted to call the FBI.

"Not from my office," Marcuse replied. She went to the office next door and made the call. Later in the day Marcuse learned that a woman had called the telephone company impersonating his wife and had ordered service shut off. At that moment he realized the seriousness of the threat. That night, while Marcuse graded papers, students in cars patrolled the neighborhood surrounding his home and stood guard with guns around the house itself. The next day, when writer Herbert Gold showed up in Marcuse's office for an interview appointment, he found the place in chaos.

"Are you the man from the FBI?" a little boy hanging around the office asked.

"No," Gold said to the child, "my hair is too long."

Marcuse's wife, Inge, appeared and, apologizing, had him turn out his pockets to make sure he wasn't armed. As soon as Marcuse's grades were turned in, the couple left for Carmel, where an old Frankfurt School colleague had offered them sanctuary.

On July 19 George W. Fisher, commander of San Diego Post 6 of the American Legion, wrote to William McGill,

UCSD chancellor, saying that Marcuse was an "admitted Marxist," and urging him not to renew the man's teaching contract for 1968—69 and to revoke Marcuse's current one. McGill refused.

The Marcuses left for Europe. His wife had been badly shaken. At UCSD it was rumored they would stay in Europe. Marcuse insisted he would return. "Quite a few students came to this place because of me," he told a reporter, "and as far as I can, I will not let them down." A special session of the UCSD faculty senate voted Marcuse their support "against the current attempts to silence him." The vote: 109-3. Thirty-two American Legion posts in San Diego County passed their own resolution demanding that Marcuse's contract be terminated and offering twenty thousand dollars to buy him out.

In France, Marcuse talked with staff members of the French magazine *L'Express*: "My own situation is precarious."

Public hostility toward Marcuse never surprised Perrin. "I always understood the way the system was going to deal with people critical of it. It bothered me from a sociological perspective, but not from a personal perspective. And I don't think it bothered him. I think he understood what was going on. He never catered to the media. I think in the end that he had the other place all the time, and that place was in the classics. He had this sense of history that put him into proper perspective."

"In San Diego to teach anything very critical would have been regarded as communistic and menacing," says Burke. "The San Diego community couldn't really tolerate this criticism."

Angry letters and hate mail poured into UCSD, to Marcuse and the administrators.

The Pacific Division of the American Philosophical Association, a professional association of philosophers, elected Marcuse its president. On the La Jolla campus, faculty continued to petition the administration to renew Marcuse's upcoming 1969—70 appointment. Even among UCSD faculty who disagreed with Marcuse's politics, the majority remained steadfast in his defense. Some of his students went to a target range and took up shooting.

In October while a blue-ribbon faculty committee investigated Marcuse, Black Panther Eldridge Cleaver addressed four thousand in the UCSD gymnasium and led them in chanting, "Fuck Ronald Reagan."

Threats against Marcuse continued through the fall. His students took turns standing guard at the door while he lectured. In the large survey courses, any person wanting to enter who was not registered in the class was searched. Ricky Sherover: "A minor scandal erupted when some dignitary wanted to come in, and I sent him to get a permission slip. But we didn't know who he was, and we weren't taking any chances."

Sherover learned to shoot. "We had target practice on Saturday afternoons, not that I was a good shot." She and several other students asked a friend, a nonstudent, if he would sit in Marcuse's large survey courses with a gun, "just in case." He did.

"He gave many public lectures. Classes were open. There may have been someone there. But it didn't matter."

The faculty committee made its report on February 3, 1969. The committee recommended reappointment. Marcuse told a reporter, "I would like to continue teaching. I don't feel that old. I feel much younger than some of my colleagues."

In Berkeley on Friday, February 21, while the Regents' late afternoon meeting was guarded by the San Francisco Police Department's Tactical Force, the Regents went into executive session to consider McGill's decision on Marcuse's reappointment. Governor Reagan spoke angrily and suggested that the power to make postretirement appointments be removed from chancellors and returned to the Regents. Moderate members of the board prevailed, however. McGill signed the letter formally notifying Professor Herberet Marcuse of his 1969–70 appointment.

June 1970. Marcuse was seventy-two. Although seventy

had become the mandatory retirement age, he was allowed to continue to teach informally. Other faculty had to sign the grades. For these one-on-one tutorials, he was not paid. There was a question about whether he should keep his office in the philosophy department on the top floor. He did. He remained a major radical figure as well, speaking out frequently amidst the incendiary events of the late sixties and seventies.

• • •

Bill Leiss, forty-seven, teaches at Simon-Frazier University in Burnaby, British Columbia. He emigrated to Canada in the late sixties, no longer able to reconcile himself with his country. He is a Canadian citizen. That so many of the students with whom Leiss associated did not carry on with an academic career, saddens him. At Brandeis and UCSD fewer than a dozen students finished a graduate degree with Marcuse. Leiss remembers the strong bond among students, first at Brandeis and then at UCSD. "It was a brief episode which was the result of very specific conditions. When it was finished, there was no trace of it. It was as if it never happened."

John Burke, forty-six now, is a counselor in the University of Washington's economics department. Every so often he and Bill Leiss and the others in the foursome get together. Ricky Sherover is often the coordinator for these meetings. In 1976, three years after the death of Marcuse's second wife Inge Neumann Marcuse, Ricky Sherover, in her early thirties, became his third wife. In 1979, after Herbert Marcuse's death in West Germany, Sherover returned to the U.S. In addition to teaching on a part-time basis at Bay Area universities, she leads workshops titled "Unlearning Racism." What was her recollection of him, his nature? "There was no secret about what he thought. Marcuse was an open book."

Ron Perrin has been teaching political science at Montana State University since 1970. He is fifty-three. Was Marcuse right in worrying about the possible price his students might pay for their association with him and for their Marxist politics? Has it cost them? Him?

"Yes. A lot of hell and agony. So in one respect he was right."

Was it worth it? (Was Marcuse worth it?)

In 1968, when he was thirty-four, Perrin had gone to Germany to work on his dissertation, corresponding regularly with Marcuse about its progress. In July 1969, Perrin and Marcuse were to meet in Paris. The day came. Perrin by then had three chapters: two on Kant and a third on Scheler.

"We had lunch," says Perrin. "I gave him the manuscript. He took it, saying, 'I'm going to get a bottle of Johnnie Walker and go up to the room and read it and meet you tomorrow.' We met the next day, went into the restaurant, and had a drink. He looked at me and said, 'You really do understand Kant, don't you? And you are the only person who made some sense out of Scheler.'"

After they parted that evening, Perrin said, "I walked the streets of Paris all night. I was in a state of absolute exhilaration—euphoric. I probably never felt any better before, or ever felt any better since. I walked across the bridges over the Seine from Left Bank to Right and back again. It was the middle of the night. No one was on the streets. I hollered and sang and danced around until five in the morning when the first trains began to leave for the suburbs where I was staying with a friend."

ROAD DOG

12

ROAD
DOG

Wiry and tense, skinny, a furze of beard and modified Afro outlining his narrow face, Tukufu had on jeans, a green polo shirt, and a Raiders cap with the bill tilted up. "I'm a street person," said Tukufu. "Primarily, my office is the front seat of my 'seventy-nine El Camino.

"Nineteen sixty-eight was my San Diego year. That's the year I had one of those rapid rises. I got sophisticated. I learned how to rob. In 1969 I went big-time—furniture stores, carpet houses, car lots. I hooked up with some other guys. I didn't want to rob nobody out of their own money. They might fight too hard for it. I wanted to rob people that had somebody else's money. I'd hit credit unions, telephone companies, gas and light companies, people who always had

—173—

cash. In a black neighborhood, there was a lot of cash back then. Black people didn't have checking accounts. Not in those days. They couldn't get 'em."

He began dealing drugs, but never used heavily. "Drugs I didn't much care for. Even in my criminal days, I needed to be in good shape. I saw my partners that messed with that heroin, they were physical wrecks, growin' old before they were supposed to.

"I am a serious believer that between seventeen and twenty-one, fear is one of the last things you have. You don't have no sense to be scared. That's how people get involved in drugs and all. You think you got a guarantee, that you got all these years to do this, and then after twenty-five, you can worry about gettin' killed. You tell yourself ever'thing is gonna take care of itself. 'I'm not gonna get shot. If I get caught, I'll just have to go jail for a while.' When I went to jail, I was considered an old man. I was twenty years old."

One of the best things that happened to him in prison was learning to play golf. "At Chino, they have a nine-hole course. We used to play for cigarettes. They were rehabilitating us. They were giving us, based on their explanation of things, some exposure of things we hadn't had. It gave me something to do other than hang with negative guys. An' I loved it. Still do. It's challenging. I play ever' chance I get.

"In December, 1970, I was convicted. I was at Chino, San Quentin, Folsom, and Susanville. I was the one that put myself into the penitentiary. I was the one who chose to run with the guys I ran with. It wasn't a hidden pressure that was snuck in on me and I just gave in to it. I made a conscious effort to be with the guys I was with. I chose to do the things I did. I suffered a lot of pain because of it. But I did it.

"We, black people, have become too hung up on materialistic concerns, too hung up in thinking we have to have so much in order to be somebody. And we start from so far behind, and we need so much before we have anything.

"Even concerned black parents don't put enough into creating the self-esteem to make a child feel he's worth something. Instead of child-rearing classes, I think black parents need classes that teach us to give our youth self-esteem, to teach them that in spite of our bein' here without nothin', they can accomplish somethin'. That's the difference between Asians who come here to this country with nothing and black folks. These people had that self-esteem.

"There's a mystique among youngsters about the other-side-of-the-law guy, the guy who hangs out in the pool hall. Those guys don't have the appearance of having a lot of restrictions on them. They have the appearance of being free and easy. I'd see them and think, 'They go. They shoot pool four—five hours, go home when they please.' I never saw them in between those times. I just assumed it was mellow. I didn't know when he wasn't at the pool hall he was maybe somewhere bein' rousted at the jail, an' maybe waitin' for somebody to come make bail.

"That thing that happens in between the glitter, that's what youngsters don' see. Take pimpin'. I used to be fascinated by a guy who could pull up, four women in the car. I mean he got out and they sat there like trained poodles. He'd send one to go to the store, he'd send one to the rib joint. Just the command he had! I'd say, 'Oooomph!'

"Every young black wants to be able to command something, because all our life we're raised to believe we're command-*less*. So I said, 'Ma-an, that's tough—to be able to do that. He's got it! A tailor-made suit on. He's got shoes on that my daddy don' even wear.'

"When you meet a guy in the street that excels your daddy, he has to be an attractive force to you. You aren't raised to follow the guy who is prudent. In a subtle way we are raised to follow after these commodities. We are taught that these trinkets, these materialistic things, are the ultimate goal for success—to be able to stack these things up and read them off: new car, new house, new sofa, new icebox, new washer and dryer. Whenever we get around a guy who seems close to that, he captivates us.

"I believe that youngsters today follow negative

influences because we've made negative influences look glamorous. It looks like a great life—wheel down the street in a pretty car, pretty girls all around you an' you, you got command over them. Ever'body beckons to you. Anybody talks to you, they talk up to you. Nobody talks down to you. You say, 'Man, I'd like to be that guy.'

"But they didn't tell you about how you be starvin', about how your ho's get taken from you, they be hungry, they sick, and they done got whupped up, a new pimp come to town and catch 'em down on the street and whup 'em up. Because soon as a new guy show up with a new car and a newer-style jewelry and a sharper suit, they gone. Nobody tells you that. They don't tell you about when your gals don't make no money. And the bottom line to pimpin' is, when your girls don' make no money, you have to make some money. You jus' can't say, 'Well, my girls aren't workin' today, I'll just do without.' Because you gotta feed 'em.

"We won't even talk about the maintenance and upkeep of a pimp's life-style. You've got to keep your car runnin' good, you've got to be able to pop ten dollars at a car wash, because that's expected of you. You may be down to your last twenty dollars, but you've got to go in there and get that ten-dollar car wash. You coulda washed it yourself, but you don't dare let someone see you washin' your own car. Because of the pimp mentality.

"It's the same with the drug dealer. All you see is the glamour. You don't see a guy pacin' the floor all night with a loaded gun because he's scared some guy is goin' to come and try to rob him. You don't see him figurin' all the security he's got to go through to move from Point A to Point B, because he thinks somebody might rip him off.

"You go to college, you learn the college system, you graduate, you get into the job world. That's a challenge. But for the guy from low economics, or no economics, the challenge quite necessarily has to be different. But all boys, regardless of color or economic possibility, in one way they're all the same. They like to do the 'I dare you's.'

"You know, 'Walk along the brick wall, balance, can you do this?' As resources take over, those challenges begin to differ. If you don't have a car, getting a car is a challenge. But if you know your daddy is going to buy you a car when you turn sixteen, the challenge becomes, 'Can I drive it at one hundred miles an hour?' If you are poor, maybe the challenge becomes to steal a car.

"I was a boy like these boys. I was a hard-core youngster. But my life was much better than theirs."

Tukufu's older brother was his parents' favorite, especially his mother's. "He played the piano. He sung church songs. I never did any of that by choice. When I did go it was for the little girls. But I had good parenting. My father laid the law down and believed that we would follow that law. He didn't believe there was any need to reiterate, 'Don't lie. Respect adults.' But there were never reasons for things. He just told you 'Do it,' he didn't say why. There was a kind of unmitigating strictness, and my mama wasn't my shade and my refuge, my port in the storm. She just wasn't.

"My first dream, from grade school on, was to be a professional baseball player, to play shortstop. The older I got, the further the reality of that dream became. I didn't see the guys with whom I could identify making it in baseball. I didn't know what the steps were. I didn't know about doing good in high school, going to college, getting exposure, learning to be all right socially. What happened is, I changed my dream. I wrote it off."

At fourteen, Tukufu had a weekend job, hauling groceries. "It provided me with money, but that's all." Until he turned fourteen, Tukufu never got into trouble. Then, he began to run with a gang. "At that age, you kinda think what you know is bein' learned for the first time. I became attracted to guys who didn't have discipline, who could do what they wanted. I wanted to be like I thought they were. I wanted a life to live of my own."

At sixteen, Tukufu graduated from high school. "I said to myself, 'I'm ready to get at the top of the world.' I went to work at a barbershop. But by then, my goal was to be a numbers runner. It wasn't runnin' those numbers that attracted me, it was how the runner was viewed by the neighborhood. You went to somebody's house to take some numbers, you got waited on as good as the preacher. Cold lemonade, all that. Maybe you got treated better. You were gonna bring some material gain, whereas, at best, the preacher was gonna bring some spiritual gain."

When he was seventeen, Tukufu got into a gang fight. Someone was knifed. Tukufu did not take part in the knifing, but he was there, he said, "cheering." He was arrested. When he came before the judge, he was given the choice of the county farm or the service. He chose the navy.

"The navy system was bad for me in the state I was in at that time. I was a rebellious person, with new-found freedom, and I didn't know what to do with it. I could do what they told me to do, and did. But when it came to governing myself, I didn't know how. I did things half-assed. My disregard for certain principles helped lead me to goin' to jail and bangin' my head for four years and eight months."

Tukufu came to the West Coast from Philadelphia when he was seventeen, to join his brother in the navy. It was 1967. "I was fascinated at that point with California guys. They were so country, and I thought they was the bravest things in the world, because they wore some of the craziest shit, shit that we thought was stage clothes. California was the first place I saw a guy, outside of a tuxedo, wearin' a ruffle shirt.

"There were certain colors we never thought a man would wear, comin' out of that East Coast culture. White pin-striped pants, white shoes to match, a white sweater. I dove off into it, head over heels. 'Cause I loved clothes. I could go down to Davison's, I could get good credit 'cause I was in the navy. I could buy top of the line. I wasn't goin' down there to that National Dollar Store.

"All the navy guys at that time stayed downtown, up in them locker clubs. Three of us rented an apartment. I got to messin' with the neighborhood women. People would say to sailors, 'Leave our girls alone, these are regular girls, girls in high school, church girls. You go downtown where those kind of girls are gravitatin', 'cause those girls are lookin' for that. I looked around downtown and I didn't see nothin' I liked."

Tukufu runs a work crew of fifteen teenage boys. He's a counselor. There were almost no black gangs in San Diego until 1969, when a member of the Los Angeles Crips moved to San Diego. He organized a chapter at Washington High School.

"San Diego's black community gets its key from Los Angeles. They set our trends. We're in the backyards of L.A. We learn from them what's uppity to do, what kind of groove you should be in. If we go to L.A. and see a truck painted up five-six different colors, the next thing you know, you see trucks in San Diego bein' painted multicolor. Same thing takes place with gang activities. Today, there are approximately seven black gangs—Lincoln Park, Piru, 5/9 Brims, West Coast, Neighborhood, Syndo, Ghosttown.

"Everybody with red on in a red neighborhood, or with blue in a blue gang neighborhood, is not necessarily a gang member. You gotta understand that these kids come along together agewise. They use the same language. They get the same likes at the same time. If some youngster starts adornin' himself in a blue hat or red shoestrings, there may be a wave of blue hats or red strings. That happens. It may not mean anything about gang membership."

In each neighborhood, the youngsters identify with the predominant neighborhood gang, or set, said Tukufu. "They use gang terminology and call each other Blood and Cuzz, but they won't necessarily get into a fight with somebody over the color of a rag hangin' off one guy's pants.

"Ever'body wants to claim something, wants to be a part of something. Gangs offer that. They also offer opportunities for advancement within the neighborhood, and recognition.

"At fourteen, a youngster starts to have value as a gang member. He has some mobility, some experiences, a certain amount of confidence. Entry-level age for gangs and for jobs is the same.

"In the black community, the primary reason kids participate in gang life is because they lack a better alternative. If a guy gets lucky, and knocks himself a job at National Steel, you won't find that guy claimin' a corner anymore. What our program tries to do is to reverse the gang process. If I have a youngster working, he begins to see people working for a living. He doesn't see jus' people who are using drugs, or peddling drugs, or sittin' all day on the porch, or trying to beat the system, or trying to claim they've got more kids in the household than they do, in order to get one over on the welfare system. When youngsters get into jobs where they see positive things going on, that's a start. They're going to learn that other stuff anyway. They're goin' to get all the teachin' from professional teachers out there on that stuff.

"For some of these guys, graduatin' from high school means more. But these guys have seen guys who didn't go to school and that make it. So there's that confusion. Here we are, society, institutions, sayin' 'Hey, you gotta go to school to be able to make it,' and then we find out that is not realistically so. 'Cause we see people that can make it.

"Like I tell these guys, I say, 'Hey, man, I know when you guys look at them guys in them pretty cars, and they're slangin' that dope, that looks good.' But I try to hurry up and let them know the other on that.

"There's some in between on that. Like when you get busted and you be up in there in that jailhouse. I done told these guys. Some of these guys go to jail, they get turned out. And I mean, quick. Some guys be too nice, too nonaggressive. So they get in one of those kind of environments, and them aggressive people get at you, and they say 'Homeboy'" —Tukufu snapped his fingers—"and the next thing you know, they have you switchin' around that tier, making fudge and drawin' Mother's Day cards. That's what they do.

"But the thing is, goin' to the pen, it's almost kinda like watchin' a guy speedin' down the street. You know it's dangerous to do, but if enough time goes by, pretty soon you'll speed. A lot of these guys, irregardless of what I've told them about the pen, and how bad it is, just by the nature of being a young man, and tryin' it for yourself, they may go that way. I think a lot of these guys think, that in terms of goin' to the pen, well, they know guys who went, and it's just one of the things that kinda makes you be cool.

"We all take after bad examples, and we follow bad influences. We do. Shucks, I looked at them guys pimpin', and drivin' those big pretty cars. You couldn't tell me that wad'nt the life to have. You couldn't drum it into me. You couldn't bring a Pope to tell me, a pretty girl to tell me, nobody could tell me that was not the life to live."

The white house on South 43rd is where the Street Youth Program has its offices. It was a beauty salon, then a doctor's office. It's one of those buildings that just becomes whatever comes along. On the wall above the doors that lead into the offices a hand-lettered sign reads:

NO RAGS, NO DRUGS
NO WEAPONS
NO GRAFFITI
OR HANDSIGNS
PERMITTED

We climbed into the Camino. Tukufu slid a cassette into the tape deck. "Patti LaBelle," he said, "she's my homegirl. She's from Philadelphia. When I was a youngster and we'd be in the basement with the red light on, slow dancin'? Her records brought me through those years. Kids don't like this stuff," he said, referring to Patti LaBelle's lush melodies and rich orchestration. "They want that rap—Run-DMC, Whodini, the Fat Boys, the Egyptian Lover. I'm gettin' old. Thirty-seven."

As we drove Tukufu pointed out neighborhood landmarks: a house where until several weeks ago a drug dealer had done business, a corner grocery where kids hung out and drugs were sold, a popular liquor store where a

—181—

drive-by killing had taken place, low-income apartment complexes. Some yards were green. There grass was glossy. Others were bare dirt. "You don't buy grass seed," said Tukufu, "when you need the money for groceries."

On walls that we passed, I saw painted: *Little Sneakaround, Little Boss Man, Big Al, Nasty Red, Mad Mike, In-sane, Mad Blue, Capone*. Tukufu said, "Can you imagine a guy namin' himself 'Little Sneakaround'? I can understand 'em wantin' to change their names, but I think it ought to be done in a different environment." (In 1969, Ben Crawley took the name "Tukufu," which means "Exalted One" in Swahili.)

As darkness fell, I saw windows glowing with lit kerosene lamps. The electricity, the gas, even the water was turned off, because people could not pay the bills. Parking lots outside low-income housing projects were lined with boys "throwing signs" with their hands. Fifteen minutes from downtown, I was in a foreign country.

"One thing about youngsters, if you explain it and at the same time offer a replacement, they'll go for it. I haven't seen nothin' these youngsters have, nothin' that they treasure or grip so tight, that they won't give it up, if you have somethin' else to offer them. What happens is that when people come, and ask 'em to give up stuff, they come with empty hands.

"They have a limited vocabulary in terms of talking about their emotions. If they don't know a guy well, they may call him 'Dude.' But if they're in the same set, an' they're friends, they'll say 'Nigger.'

"Their English sometimes gets them diagnosed as developmentally disabled. If you took me and dumped me in China, I'm sure I'd be developmentally disabled. A lot of that clinical talk—'Well, Johnny, your apprehension of things is faulty'—that don't go over with these youngsters.

"These kids aren't that different than anybody else's kids. They don't have a cow to kick and a watermelon patch to go steal a watermelon from, so they go write some graffiti on somebody's wall. I used to think that only blacks did this. Hell, white boys do this, too."

Liko Davis. Stocky, neatly dressed and almost dapper, he displays an obdurate, oxlike patience and a smile that starts slowly and then hangs on through a conversation. Born and reared in San Diego County by hard-working parents, his father a janitor and his mother a schoolteacher, a self-described middle-class kid who drifted into trouble, "drawn into crime by the lure of easy money."

The first ten years of his life Davis lived in La Jolla. "To me, twenty years ago, La Jolla seemed quiet and sedate, while the Southeast rolled with excitement. There were house parties every night, and the time folks went to bed in La Jolla was the time folks got up in the Southeast."

Davis became a gang member, a Vice Lord, at fourteen. He got into drugs: "sniffin' airplane glue, then from glue to pills to LSD." He fought. "I got shot four times, stabbed twice, got a plate in the back of my head from where I got hit with a baseball bat, got a scar across my nose from a switchblade." He was lucky enough, because although he got into drug-dealing—heroin, cocaine, PCP, marijuana—he quickly got into and out of heavy drug use. "Drugs were like drinking, for me. I couldn't handle either. I'd get so sad, and I'd just start cryin', when I was drunk or high, thinkin' about my mother. Guys would say to me, 'Liko, you're no fun.' I liked living on the edge, and before I knew it, I had caught myself up in a spiderweb of something that was a nightmare: trial, conviction, almost nine years in prison.

"They gave me those aptitude tests, for placement. I said, 'Boy, I'm gonna do real well, so maybe I can get a good job, or maybe they'll send me to a prison without all the violence.' When I got to San Quentin, Big Red Nelson was the warden. He was a big Oklahoma redneck, red as a beet, red as meat, fire-engine-red hair, six feet and six inches and weighing two twenty-five, not an ounce of fat on him, lean, mean. He acted just like he was a prisoner, as opposed to a warden. We met. He was lookin' at my test scores. He said, 'You know, there's two things I hate. One's dogs that chase cars and the other is educated niggers.' Then he said, 'What do you want to do, 'cause you gonna be here a long time.' I said, 'Well, warden, I'd like to be an electrician.' He laughed, said, 'We're gonna make you a cook.' All the blacks worked in the kitchens, Chicanos worked in the laundry, whites had the clerical positions. So, I cooked. Culinary, they called it.

"Prison gave me a chance to look at myself, to do some introspection. Prison was a nightmare, but it was also the best thing that ever happened to me in my life."

Davis finished high school in prison, and after he got out, he attended college. Before he came to the Street Youth Program, Davis, whose area of expertise is drug-abuse prevention, worked with Crash, Inc., a San Diego substance-abuse treatment facility. Here at the Street Youth Program, he counsels youngsters with drug problems. He makes many contacts for the program by offering drug-education presentations at schools and churches in the program target areas. Davis has also served as consultant and speaker for the Bank of America, General Dynamics, and Rohr. It was during his incarceration that Davis got into public speaking. He laughed, ruefully. "Most of the guys in prison couldn't read or write. I'd read to them. I'd put all this drama into the story, these gestures. Guys, big guys, thugs, would follow me around, like little kids. They'd say, 'Hey, Liko, read this! Read this!' "

The average age at which kids begin to use drugs is twelve and one-half. "PCP," Davis said. "It's use is especially prevalent in black communities. It is cheap and readily available, easier to get than a six-pack of beer, because with the beer, a kid at least has to find an adult to buy it for him.

"Like, when I was coming up, we took PCP, but it was orally ingested in a pill form. Today, kids smoke PCP. When I was coming up, you injected cocaine or sniffed it. Today people smoke it, freebase it.

"Cocaine is one of those drugs that makes you feel euphoric, hyperalert, hyperaware, filled with initiative, drive, enthusiasm. All those American things, it makes you feel them. That's how people get into it. I don't care how successful you are or how big a failure you are. Cocaine gives you attributes we all admire and would like to have naturally. The thing about it, though, 'What comes up, must go down.'

"Adolescents, particularly in poor communities, tend to measure success by what a man drives and how he dresses. Kids see dealers dressing in tailor-made suits and driving brand-new cars. Guess what they are influenced to do? Then they look at a poor social worker who drives a used car and buys his clothes off the rack."

Most of our clients come from families whose incomes fall below the poverty line. Few fathers live in the household. Some boys are fathers themselves. Typically, they lead very isolated lives. Many rarely, if ever, leave the area. I had supposed that they watched a lot of television.

"No," said Davis, "they just sleep. And then when night comes, and they can't sleep anymore, they prowl the neighborhood.

"It's really sad, because they're intelligent and perceptive. But they are victims of poor teachers who aren't sensitive to minorities and parents who are ignorant." Many can barely speak standard English. "And English, for them," said Davis, "is not a second language!"

"They have experienced so much failure, that when you ask them what kind of work they're lookin' for, they'll say, 'Can you get me a janitor's job? Can I pull weeds somewhere?' "

Tukufu was upset. An old "running partner," his "road dog," had been shot in a drive-by killing. His assailant was unknown, Tukufu said.

"Your road dog, he's the guy, he's got two dollars when you go to eat an' you know you got a buck when the time comes to pay."

Liko Davis had just heard of a friend's suicide. It seemed somebody here was always dying, and dying young. Tukufu pointed to a stack of black-bordered funeral service programs on his desk. On the cover of each leaflet was a name and a photograph of a black male face. Young faces, each with its own peculiar stamp of particular sweetness. One had big, long-lashed eyes. Another had a lopsided gap-tooth grin, a little space between his teeth.

Obituaries were printed on page two. The young men came from large families. Some had fourteen sisters and brothers; others had eight, six, nine. I calculated the ages at which the men had died. The oldest had been twenty-two, the youngest seventeen. One obituary: " 'Bake Nuts,' as he was affectionately known, by his family and friends, enjoyed playing football and basketball in his spare time. He was a loving and caring person.

"One who had a warm smile and a pleasing personality."

The death of "Bake Nuts" was described as "untimely," the time and place of death as "Sunday evening at a local hospital." On the back page, a poem: "Do not stand at my grave and weep / I am not there. I do not sleep. / I am a thousand winds that blow. / I am the diamond glints on snow. / I am the sunlight on ripened grain. / I am the gentle autumn rain. / Do not stand at my grave and cry. / I am not there. I did not die."

How had Bake Nuts died?

"Gang-related."

Tukufu was listed as a pallbearer in several leaflets. "I can't count anymore how many times I been a pallbearer," he said. "There's a whole batch of kids I'm not seeing now, kids that are older, that are high-school dropouts. I try to get them into entry-level employment and back into school. If I hear they're hiring at Ryan, and I have three kids who seem ready to get into that, I will work with them. In the wintertime, I do more going to them. I do more one-on-one sessions. I do more pickin' up guys, puttin' them in the car, and ridin' them around. You know, 'C'mon man, what you doin'?' 'Aw, I ain' doin' nothin'.' 'Well, come on,' I'll say, 'I got a little action on some job. Let's go look at it and then pick us up some lunch.'

"Believe me, when you take one of those youngsters and allow him to be in your car, he feels like you've given him something. They go back to their buddies an' say, 'Kufu let me go in the Camino.' 'Kufu let me sport the Camino.'

"I am amazed at these youngsters, at their bein' able to make it this far. They are more than me. I believe they can excel. I want to make 'em feel, 'They're things that I can do other than those which is most prominent in my eyesight.' I want to make 'em feel that the world is gigantic. Because it is."

BLUE PLATE BLUES

13

BLUE
PLATE
BLUES

Food carries memories. I've suspected that the reason we have a fondness for foods foreign to us is, in part, that they *don't* carry *our* memories. But what about the nostalgia for distinctively American food, for home cooking, square meals, and blue-plate specials?

In 1944, the next-to-last summer of the war—my age: three, going on four—my mother tosses my father out and takes me to her mother in Arkansas. My grandmother works a shipwreck of a farm on forty hilly acres in the northern part of the state. When my mother hikes her skirt above her stocking tops to pull herself up into the rusted-out pickup at the crest of the drive, I do not know I will not see her again until two months before my sixth birthday. I break out in boils anyway.

My grandmother is sixty-five in '44. Twenty years earlier, she had chucked my mother's father, a Folger's coffee salesman, in Indianapolis, left off my then six-year-old mother in a Roman Catholic convent in Albuquerque, and followed her man ("My man, I love him so," she sang low in the belly, "I'll never let him go") to Los Angeles, where they opened a popcorn stand near the La Brea tar pits, and then on to the Klondike in Alaska, where they panned for gold. Since the late thirties, she has lived alone on the farm with her two hired hands, Bushels and Buckles.

I call her Grammy. This little squat tub of a woman. She is brutal, powerful, and repulsive. She never feeds me a bad meal.

On the red-checkered gingham tablecloth Grammy sets down meals that stick to the ribs and do not hide the hard facts of the heavy thingness of things. Her cooking does not conceal being born, hard work, and bloody death; does not deny its roots; does not smother its origins in sauces. It smells like itself. It uses lard, thick cream, the fatback off the hog, and butter, yellow cornmeal, and flour that comes in cloth sacks from which tea towels and children's nighties are made. It is mixed with the hands and fried in iron skillets.

Nothing goes to waste. When Grammy butchers hogs she pickles the cloven feet (trotters), the pointed, cartilaginous ears, and the curling bone-and-gristle tails. She packs head cheese into the long-snouted hog's head. Any pork remnants she grinds down into sausage, which she stuffs into the hog's intestines. The last renderings and bacon grease, hoarded over the months in Mason jars, she turns into a smoke-blackened iron pot of swilling lye to make soap.

Milk is never let go bad. What Bushels and Buckles do not haul up to the road in sweating metal jugs for the dairy driver to pick up, what we do not drink, what is not poured into a trough for the piglets, Grammy churns into butter, makes into egg custards and puddings. She separates curds from whey, hangs the curds out on the clothesline in a cheesecloth clabber bag. More whey drips on the ground. On the table the next day, there is a bowl of soured clabber milk whose tender pebble curds you strew with sugar.

It is slow food, somebody's-at-home food, and takes its time on back burners and low flames. Cooked vegetables are overcooked. The liquid left in the pot after cooking vegetables is called pot likker and coats your mouth with a taste that is mineral, dark and green, musty. You dip squares of cornbread or rolled-up slices of light bread in the pot likker.

There is breaded tomato, made from tomatoes canned in August. Pools of melted butter percolate out from the khaki bread crusts onto a lake of tomato juice. It is like eating scenery.

Grammy stands in the walk-in pantry and gazes at her Mason jars packed with whole pickled peaches stuck with cloves, bread-and-butter pickle, lye-soaked pale green and paler pink watermelon-rind pickle, golf-ball-size pickled beets, pickled okra pods with frills of dill head. Standing with her hands on her broad hips, she will count the quarts of Bing cherries, white Royal Annes, boysenberries, pie cherries, cling peach halves, and whole ivory Seckel pears, stem on, suspended in clear juice. When her best friend, Stell Ellis, comes to visit from Springfield, Missouri, Stell will say to my grandmother, "Let me look at your canning, doll."

In the iron pot, a stewing hen floats and bobs in her own bubbling juices. Her goose-bumped skin sweats yellow fat. Grammy had scooped out from the hen's mysterious jumble of guts, gizzard, liver, and gravel, a handful of embryonic eggs with yolks no bigger than marbles and has set them aside for gravy. As the hen simmers, her wings slowly loosen at the joint and lay out on either side of her high-peaked breast like blunted angel wings on the gold-flecked broth, and the pure white dumplings puff up into summer clouds.

Grammy makes pork roast in the iron roaster while I think of how the witch tried to fatten up Gretel for her oven. I see if I can still measure my wrist with my thumb and finger. I can, and while I rest in the knowledge that I am not yet oven-ready, Grammy, who sings but never whistles while she works ("A whistling woman, a cackling hen, will always come to some bad end," she warns), Grammy fries apple rings in butter until the apples are see-through as dime-store blouses.

At night all four of us—me and Grammy and Bushels and Buckles—eat together. I suspect that our main meal came at four-thirty rather than at the traditional noontime of most farms because Grammy worked as long as her hired men.

My grandmother grew up, she would tell me, as the oldest child—"mother to my mother's young'ns"—in a large German immigrant family, on a farm in Indiana, "working my fingers to the bone." Her mother was stern and hard—by all accounts, a scrawny, puny, mean-hearted little woman—and Grammy ran away at sixteen. She married my uncle's father, "a dreamer," and left him for the Folger's coffee salesman who became my mother's father, and then when my mother turned six, left him, too. My mother, who would not permit me to see my father, never saw her father again after that.

"It would have been disloyal even to ask," my mother says, eyeing me meaningfully.

"Didn't you want to see him?" I ask.

"That is irrelevant," she answers.

My mother and father eloped. Grammy and my father were enemies from the start of my parents' eight-year marriage. Grammy minces no words: He is "no good," my "spoiled, rich-kid father." I am "his spitting image," she says, waggling her butcher knife so close to my nose that my eyes almost cross and I can see the upper denture shift in her mouth.

I learned sass from my father, Grammy says. And I inherited bad habits, like "playin' with your nasty self," she tells me, laughing and wrathful all at once. "You're pig as any, girl."

I will end up, she warns, like the neighbor's silly boy. He "played his nasty." If she catches me at it, she will do what her mother did—sprinkle red pepper on my "nasty."

Grammy, like her daughter, beat me unmercifully with anything that happened to be at hand. And it was from

Grammy, who in repose appeared jolly, that my mother—as smoothly beautiful as a cameo—learned to say "I'm gonna cut the blood out of you."

I see Grammy, to this day, by the back porch. A feed-sack apron covers the navy-blue white-polka-dot dress. She holds her butcher knife like a scepter and says "cheese" when her two children tell her to; the grin is not hers. She is four-feet, ten-inches tall—"stout," my mother says when she shows a friend the snapshot. (Now that Grammy is long dead my mother regards her mother as picturesque. "Quaint," my mother says. In truth Grammy was big as a house, forty-five, maybe fifty inches at the belly. She was what she would have called a "Man Mountain Dean.") Her narrow eyes peer out of the photograph from between pillows of fat. Even her pierced earlobes are fat—and twinkle with diamond studs. Her face is an effeminate George Washington. She could be his sister. Her skin hangs in folds off her square jawline, her lips gathered like a coin purse.

Once a week she rinses her white hair with laundry bluing. (The blue brought out the blue of her eyes, explains my mother many years later in a rhapsodic contralto, as if she had forgotten the facts of her own life, forgotten that she says to me when she turns forty, "I would never have divorced your father, you know, had it not been for your grandmother.") Dirt works, down deep, into the lines across Grammy's palms. Her hands are callused. She never wears gloves. "I can't grab hold good," she says.

Orange bunions bulge on her size-five feet. For years she has worn ill-fitting shoes and boots. After her bath she sits on her bed, a folded towel under one foot. She cuts at her bunions with a straight razor. One night she slices too deeply. Her blood turns the white towel pink.

Before she switches off her lamp at night she soaks her dentures, which rub open sores on her gums, in a glass of water mixed with baking soda. Then she takes two tablespoons of pink Pepto-Bismol for her sour stomach. Under her pillow there is a sheathed dagger and a blue-black .38.

Grammy works unbelievably hard. Year-round, she milks at dawn and dusk, rubbing the cows' udders afterward with "bag balm"; shovels out manure and spreads fresh hay; waters and feeds cows, chickens, horses, mules; slops the hogs, summoning them with a gusty "*Soooeeee, soooeeee,* pig"; midwifes cows and hogs. Once spring comes, she has the garden, the canning, the baby chicks mailed to her from the hatchery, and piglets. And when all that is done, she comes in, sighing, through the screened-in back porch, swearing about the hired hands, or a cow, a mule, a calf, or at me. She pulls off her rubbers and ties on her apron and begins the housework: laundry (ours and the hands'), cooking, baking, cleaning up. I follow behind her to fetch, pick up, dust, and fold, to iron handkerchiefs, pit and peel, snap beans, shell peas, hull strawberries.

She raises pullets, fryers, and the heavy-breathing laying hens under whose hot breasts I stick my hand to gather eggs. In summer, I get chicken shit between my bare toes. Grammy keeps russet Jersey milk cows who moan right before milking time, their bags are so full. Then she squats down on the stool, her legs wide apart, her blued hair rising and falling along the red flank. Humming, she works down the teat. Afterward, the empty bags sway when the cows walk out of the dark barn.

At farrowing time, rolling up her sleeves, she reaches clear to her elbow into an agonized laboring sow and tugs. She grabs the delicate foretrotters and waits for another grunt, another contraction. A convulsive heave raises the sow's head off the new straw and out pops a piglet, the fetal membrane hooding its snout and pressing its ears flat against its skull. She pulls back the membranous sac as easily as I peel a banana, and vigorously pumps the piglet's back legs until it takes its first breath and squeals. "They are eating the buttons off their mother's vest," Grammy tells me when the piglets each root in at a teat and begin to nurse. Because she leers, I think this is a dirty joke. I repeat it, years later, in the schoolyard. Everyone laughs.

She keeps two horses, a white stallion and a dray, or draught horse, and a succession of sorry spavined mules who truculently pull plows, a semimechanical seeder, a clanking rusted harrow. Her milk separator takes cream from milk and an electric churner churns butter. She puts on her glasses and reads farm sale lists. She goes to auctions.

She sows field corn, alfalfa, and sweet clover, puts in hillocks of Country Gentleman roasting ears, and rows of staked-up Kentucky Wonder green beans, and I tear strips of worn-out sheet to tie up the bean vines. She raises beefsteak tomatoes, round hummocks of red potatoes, Charleston Gray watermelons that she sends Bushels to cool in the creek.

Bushels and Buckles call Grammy, whose given name is Beatrice, "Mrs. Roberts," and "ma'am." Where fat Bushels and scrawny Buckles got their names, no one says. White-haired, grizzle-chinned, piss-smelling old men, they shave on Friday night and on Saturday change to clean blue overalls that are baggy but do not hide their bowlegs. Their hands are missing digits and their mouths missing teeth. When I can count I learn that, between the two men, they have three whole thumbs and thirteen and one-half fingers. They get blood blisters and toothaches and Bushels says he has a kidney stone. After lunch they sit with their legs splayed out and their hands fanned out over their crotches. ("Never show them your business," Grammy says.)

They bunk out back behind the chicken house and cow barn in a cabin heated by a wood cookstove and papered with Little Rock *Gazettes.* They use a one-seater outhouse behind the cabin. ("Never go in there. You get disease," Grammy says.)

They never mention family. They don't ever say "back home." They don't talk much at all. Grammy studies Buckles, his narrowed-down eyes watching the mist rising on the back pasture, and says, "That fella squints just like a suck-egg dog."

Grammy assures anyone who asks that the hands are widowers. But she tells people she is a widow woman. Even I know she isn't. What she is was what she, sneering, would call a "grass widow."

Grammy is the first person I see naked. Her yellow-white pubic hair springs up like dying grass across drooping purple labia. The corset ribbing cuts red vertical ridges into her rib cage, her flow of belly, her thighs. Her long loose breasts—she calls them "dinners"—are striped with stretch marks and tipped with nubby beige corduroy nipples. Her clabbered-milk thighs, her drooping buttocks—"hind-end," she says—the wild swatches of white hair growing from her armpits: I study her body as a palm reader might pause at a break in your lifeline. At sundown she stands in the bathtub and washes with a scratchy gray bar of lye soap. After she dries off, she shakes out white clouds of Cashmere Bouquet onto the yellowed skin on which the "dinners" rest. She rubs the talcum into the hair under her arms and into the hair covering her sex, and then she wriggles on the flesh-pink sateen underpants she calls "drawers."

Her biceps are the size of a man's. She is incredibly strong. I watch as she "sticks," dresses out, and butchers a series of behemothic, struggling, squealing hogs. A hog, I learn, is a pig that weighs more than 120 pounds, and Grammy estimates that three hogs weigh half a ton. Both of them straining, she and one of the hired men will hoist a carcass onto an ancient tree limb reinforced with two-by-fours. The body hangs, snout down. The limb bows and groans. The blood pools, gums up in the red dirt. The flies buzz loudly. In the midst of dribbling blood and circling flies, with her George Washington features smooth and calm, she saws, blade scraping against bone. Hams, loins, racks of ribs. She chops off the same trotters I watched her, months ago, pump to get the pig to take its first breath.

She severs chickens' necks as easily as she dices a carrot. She places the fluttering chicken on the oak stump in the backyard, chops off its head with a prompt whack of the ax, then tosses the decapitated body onto the ground for the dust-raising rumpus she calls "the last dance." She pitches to the dog the red-combed head, and its eyes—seconds ago as bright as a new doll's—begin to film. (When she screams, as she often does, "You are going to the dogs," the expression carries deadly significance.) Gripping its yellowed feet, she plunges the chicken carcass into boiling water to loosen the feathers and, then outside (behind the backyard if there is a wind), feathers fly while she plucks.

• • •

Some extravagant strain in Grammy goes beyond tooth-and-claw survival. One day out in the pasture to the west of the house, she castrates a gray-mottled white stallion—"young Cholly"—who has kicked her, she swears, "for the last time." Cholly's rib cage does accordion wheezes and, with each deflation, another flush of magenta blood floods the tall grass. His high moans chill the hot summer air. "I struck a damn artery, boys," she says to Bushels and Buckles, who look at the ground.

Finally, she has to shoot him. The silent trio, each with a shovel, dig next to Cholly's mounded white body. Before they push him in, Grammy—wearing her high-top boots—kicks the horse and, with her fist raised, screams, "You goddamn son of a bitch, I'd do it to you again if I could!"

One night in '43 she killed a "Comanchee Injun." She loves to tell the story. "You see, I heard somebody tryin' to start my son's Packard coupe up out in the garage along about three in the ayem, an' I creeped out there in my bare feet and nightie [she wears nightgowns that she sews from gauzy feed sacks, and as I outgrow and wear out the clothes I came with, they are replaced with feed-sack dresses], pickin' up the icepick on my way. It was pitch black in the garage, an' he never saw me comin', so busy he was tryin' to hot-wire that coupe. I just put the ol' pick right in his back and before he could even straighten up good, I got him a second jab."

Depending on her audience and her mood, she will supply the short, expurgated or long and unexpurgated version—a *vision* in either instance of unrelieved bloody slaughter—and in the unexpurgated she will triumphantly wave the blood-spotted feed-sack nightgown in her listener's face. Then comes the coda: "When the sheriff and his boys got here, they told me that Injun had a record miles long, and had escaped without them even knowin' it from the county work farm just across the hill.

"I'd guess," she always adds, studying her audience's eyes, "they talked about that over at the county farm for a long time!"

(As a child I believed she loved killing, that she was a Nazi of the barnyard, conducting her spectacular pogroms against the hooved, the horned, the curly-tailed and spotted, the web-footed and speechless. Hacking at a hog's leg to get at what would be smoked into ham, blood running, dripping off her wrists, she once looked across at me, my eyes covered with my hands, and hollered, "Even the devil's got to eat.")

By 1944 over seven million men are in uniform. On June 6 the Allies land in Normandy and by mid-July the U.S. Pacific forces overrun Saipan. Grammy's favorite of her two children, my uncle, is with the navy on Okinawa. One afternoon she pushes aside the heavy ivory lace curtains and licks the back of a war mother's sticker—a white star on a field of azure blue—and glues it to her front window.

To me, the war pours as naturally through life as the tap water from the deep well out back. But war is also a bogeyman, evil and dangerous, whose face I cannot and do not imagine.

War is Japs. When the news was bad, she would say "when they attack the farm, they will float down on us"—her stubby fingers illustrate the plunge—"with parachutes. They will catch you and stick you"—she mimes the Japs' short stabs and my grunts—"in the belly with a bayonet. Then they will cook you in the big pot in the yard, and eat you with the pickles." All dark-skinned people, she tells me, like hot, spicy food and are cannibals.

Any distant flash of heat lightning, every far-off rattle of thunder, any backfire out on the road, might be the bombs she prophesied. Every hyperexcited voice rising through the Philco's static could be its herald. "Shut up, young'n" she commands while she tunes.

• • •

Grammy came from people and from a generation that had gone hungry. War evokes her fear of going hungry again. She smokes hams and sides of bacon for Mr. Black—the euphemism for the black market—to trade for rationed tires, for the sugar and coffee she hoards. We do not butcher beef, so, under the counter, she trades a side of pork with a butcher for a side of beef.

When she uses the tough round steaks, she takes out the clawhammer and beats them out thin to make chicken-fried steak. She pours a half cup of flour, two tablespoons of salt, and a pinch of black pepper into a brown paper bag. One at a time, she puts the steaks into the bag, shaking it up and down until the meat is thoroughly coated. When the melted lard in the iron skillet is hot enough that a drop of water tossed skilletward pops, it is time to put in the steaks. She cooks them on one side until the blood seeps up to the top, then flips them over. How long she cooks them depends on whether she wants the meat rare or well done, the coating crisp or mushy. For Bushels and Buckles, she cooks it mushy and adds, right before taking the steaks out of the skillet, several dollops of Worcestershire sauce, which she pronounces "Warchess-tire." She always leaves any pieces of crust that fall off the steaks in the skillet to give the gravy "crunchers."

Grammy makes our bread. She kneads up mounds of dough and puts it in a floured bowl under a clean dishrag to rise. Before the bread is finished baking, she rubs the tops with melted butter to brown the crust. She makes yeast rolls, cinnamon rolls, and, in the winter, apple kuchen. She makes fresh buttermilk biscuits and cornbread. To the cornbread recipe off the sack, she sometimes adds a pint jar of home-canned creamed corn or, better, she stands three or four fresh ears on a plate, slices the kernels from the cobs with her butcher knife, and scrapes the kernels and the "milk" from the cut corn into her cornmeal mixture. Or she will crumble bacon left from breakfast or "cracklins" saved from rendering a hog.

• • •

The war dominates the news, but polio comes next. Polio had paralyzed Roosevelt while he was governor of New York, and in 1944 it kills over one thousand people, even more in 1945, and cripples additional thousands. In newspapers, between the lean-jawed generals, the pale dying boys, and the bombers with noses painted to look like dragons, I stare at polio victims in "iron lungs" and Sister Kenny briskly massaging atrophied limbs. If I have even the slightest sore throat (a polio symptom), I am too scared to tell Grammy.

"Polio"—and the "silly boy" who rides his white mule past our house—is the reason Grammy gives when she says no when I ask to play with the children down the road. Excepting occasional Saturday afternoons when we ferry the delicate eggs at ten miles per hour around high-shouldered furrows left by farm wagons, I do not leave the farm.

Grammy "sets" on the back porch, snapping and stringing green beans. These are times when she tells me about growing up in Indiana. She grabs the bean string on the stem end, where the bean flower once was, and pulls downward. The string comes off. She pinches off the ends. Then she snaps the bean in two. Right after lunch, she cooks up a mess of beans for that night's supper.

To make her green beans, she chops thick-sliced bacon or fatback into half-inch cubes, which she puts in a heavy pot with snapped and stringed beans and two chopped yellow onions. (She also adds any beet or turnip tops or any other tender greens—spinach, mustard—she has on hand. Tiny turnips, thinned from the garden, are plopped in whole and are particularly delicious.) After barely covering them with water, she simmers the beans on a back burner for an hour or two until they turn a dark olive green in color and are mushy in texture. The pot likker is served in a sauce bowl.

Grammy subscribes to *Country Gentleman,* the *Saturday Evening Post,* a local Sunday newspaper, and although she was not a Jehovah's Witness, her friend Stell Ellis is, and Stell sees to it that my grandmother gets *The Watchtower* every week. But Grammy never reads it. She gets seed catalogues and invitations to farm sales and saves them all. The drawer of her library table is stuffed with crisp, yellowed, illustrated pamphlets on colon diseases, colonic irrigation, rupture and hernia cures and hernia trusses, letters from my mother and uncle. She owns a navy-blue leatherette Bible, a Webster's dictionary my uncle won as a college prize, a mildewed copy of Robert Service's *The Cremation of Sam McGee*—probably a remnant from her Klondike days—and a catalogue with tipped-in reproductions of Degas's ballet dancers—sent by my uncle—from the Metropolitan Museum of Art. About that catalogue, she tells me, "That's where your mother lives."

When I have been good, when the war news is hopeful, the hens laying well, the Jerseys giving milk with a high cream content, Grammy lets me have the "toe-dancer pictures." I sit on the davenport in winter or, in summer, on the porch swing and gaze at Degas's pastels, the filmy blue tutus, pink-suffused faces, and tight chignons—"topknots" she calls them, and if I beg she will make one in my hair. But, she warns, "Don't expect me to do this every day. You're the kind that give 'em an inch, they take a mile."

When she is down at the barn or out in the field or vegetable garden, I go to her bedroom, a shady, cool room centered around a vast mahogany four-poster, crowded with massive matching chests of drawers on which she has placed starched tatted "runners" and, against the walls, cardboard boxes in which she stores clothing from what she remembers as her "better days" and gunnysacks stuffed with rags for rag rugs. I stand in front of the long mirror built into the door to her wardrobe closet and, lifting my feed-sack skirts with one hand and with the other pulling back my hair for a topknot—in the boys' boots that Grammy buys me (I do not dare take them off because I can't tie the laces)—I try to stand on my toes.

· · ·

The two-foot-high Philco, shaped like an arch in a cathedral and covered, across the front, with brown fabric, carries war news, Roosevelt's Saturday night "fireside chats," hillbilly music, "Queen for a Day," "Our Gal Sunday," farm reports. Just before supper on the 23rd of April 1945—by which time I have, through a series of maneuvers, taught myself to read—FDR's death is announced on the radio. For the next eighty-five hours, only grief mixed with the static. Grammy stops dead. She sobs. She beats the green wool easy chair. "It's like I was widowed myself," she sobs to Bushels and Buckles, who look frightened over the bowls of bread torn up in milk that is our dinner that night. The next morning Grammy, wiping her eyes on the corner of her apron, walks slowly down the steep grade to the barn to milk Bossy, Joan Crawford, Clabber Girl, and Vanessa. She has looped a black sateen armband around her thick upper arm. She hates Harry Truman. Not until Stell Ellis shows up after Decoration Day does Grammy cheer up. Stell and Grammy have been "pals forever." Stell comes three to four times a year. Stell is married to a bookkeeper for the city of Springfield and has three daughters. Two of their husbands are in the war. The third has asthma. One daughter is "no-'count," and from what I overhear, Stell has worries with her husband—"the old goat"—who has "prostrate trouble" and is "chasin' young tail."

Stell drives a black Ford with leather seats down Route 66, which she grimly calls "Blood Alley." Her husband gets her extra gas coupons from "Mr. Black."

Stell wears bright lipstick and matching cheeks. She shaves her eyebrows and then in the morning draws them on with a pencil. The pencil matches her "good" hair, which, when I ask, she tells me is "hennaed and marcelled at the beauty parlor." She rubs deodorant cream in her shaved armpits. The deodorant is called "Odor-o-no" and comes in a cobalt-blue glass jar. She dabs on a strong perfume: hyacinth, she says. She wears what Grammy calls a "ruched and tucked" dress with "gussets," and has, she admits, when Grammy compliments her, "a cute figure." Grammy uses "the Haviland" instead of the "kitchen dishes" when Stell visits, and she is all dressed up, too — in silk or rayon jersey dresses clasped at the bosom with a brooch, and high-heel black pumps.

For two to three days, Grammy leaves the farm work, even the milk cows, to Bushels and Buckles while she and Stell drink coffee and talk. Stell always gives Grammy a permanent, and it is always "too goddamn tight."

One day Stell runs her hand through my natural — and tight — curls, and says to my grandmother, "Doesn't she just have hair like a nigger, though, Beatrice?"

Grammy laughs until she cries, and says, "She sure does. Now wouldn't that be funny though?"

Once, while Stell waits for Grammy's permanent to set, she tells me about her grandson, Bobby, her "eldest," whose "belly button wasn't tied up right tight at birth, you know, missy?" Stell, like my grandmother (who calls me "young'n" and "girl"), never calls me by name. One day when Bobby was six he ate too much of Stell's angel cake and peach ice cream and "burst his guts out onto the living-room carpet." According to Stell, her fast action in "scooping the guts back up into him" with her bare hands is what saved the boy's life.

When Stell gets ready to leave, Grammy and Bushels and Buckles load her down with farm goods. Grammy packs blocks of the butter she churns with the electric churner into cheesecloth, carefully tilts the brown eggs Stell favors into egg cartons, takes down a side of bacon from its iron hook in the smokehouse and folds it into newspapers, arranges jars of cling peaches, green beans, kraut into orange crates and, if it is summer or fall, the two women get out early, roll their hose around their knees and hitch up their skirts with clothespins, and pick "messes" of corn, green beans, ripe tomatoes, long shiny eating cukes, and little, nubby, hard-warted picklers, yellow crookneck squash, okra, the netted-rind muskmelons, and pale green honeydews.

As soon as one laundry basket is heaped, I struggle up through the rows, dodging the humming mosquitoes that rise up right after first light. I thread through strands of scratchy hollyhocks and sidestep the sharp edges of the colossal drooping sunflower heads, and, grunting with the weight of the basket, the wire handles digging into and cutting my palms, I say to myself, sweating and red-faced, "Chug-a-chug-chug; I am the little engine that could."

Then Stell is ready to go. She and Grammy hug and kiss and cry. Stell tells me, "You help out your grandmother, you hear?" She honks and waves as she backs out of the driveway and Grammy directs her. Stell's flowers stand up in jars wedged into the front seat with melons and corn and cabbages. Grammy has a scarlet cupid-bow lipstick mark on her doughy powdered cheek. She stands up at the road by the mailbox until all she sees of Stell Ellis is dust. That is what she says when she gets back to the yard. "I stood out there until all I could see of Stell Ellis was dust." She is blinking back tears, and her face looks bigger under the new tight curls.

During World War II, those who can raise Victory Gardens and, generally, eat more vegetables. It is not unusual for families to have two, three, even four vegetables at a main meal. In summer we eat green beans, crookneck squash, fried okra, and mashed potatoes and turnip. The yellow crookneck squash is not only aesthetically pleasing but has a far sweeter taste than zucchini. After slicing four squash and one yellow onion in rings, Grammy simmers them (with just enough water to cover them in the pan) until the vegetables are soft. After straining off the pot likker (preferably into a pan of green beans), she mashes the squash and onions with a potato masher until the vegetables start to break up. "Directly" before serving, Grammy adds one-half of a quarter-pound stick of butter to the cooked vegetables in the pan along with a couple of tablespoons of sugar and a sprinkling of salt and pepper.

When she fixes mashed potatoes, Grammy adds to the raw potatoes one medium-size turnip, sliced. Grammy frequently complains that "city cooks" will whip potatoes until they are the consistency of wallpaper paste. "Mashed potatoes, goddamn it, means mashed."

Although I did not know it in 1944 or '45, or did not know the name for what I felt, I know now that I was unrelievedly lonely. I missed my mother, who was working on her master's degree in New York. I learned not to.

"When is Mama coming for me?"

She says (if she answers me at all), "I don't know," or, "If she gets married again, her new husband may not want you." Once she tells me, holding a letter from my mother in her hand and looking up over the top of her spectacles, "Your mama has her a soldier boy."

I hardly dared permit myself to think of my father. When I tried to conjure my father mentally, he was dim—long shadow and heat. I remember only warmth and hugeness. I knew he was bad. I suspected I was like him.

I have dolls, Belinda and Pearly and George. I pat out mud pies for them mixed with rocks and eggs I steal out of the hen house, and peach peels and apple parings I get from the pig slops when I carry them down.

I teach Grammy's dog to bring down hens. By screaming "Sic 'im, sic 'im," I get him to grab the chickens in his mouth. Their squirming and pecking excites him, and he worries at their necks until he wears them down. When the hen ceases flapping, squawking, pecking, he wearies of the game and lumbers off, feathers sticking to his muzzle, and leaves the heaving half-dead chicken.

I felt a disorienting pleasure, watching the dog tear at a hen. But once he has walked off, I swear to never do it again, and try to erase the event from my mind. (Ever after I will feel a commonality, a chilly familial bonding, with mass murderers, idle snipers, and movie villains.)

For a long time Grammy is mystified by the mauled chickens. Finally, she catches me, out by the blackberry bushes, which grow as thick as concertina wire, and I think hide me from view. She catches me siccing the hound on a black-and-white speckled pullet.

Grammy grabs me up by the hair and switch whips me until I run blood. Often when she punishes me, she says, "Why don't you just git to your mother in New York," and during this whipping she repeats her suggestion—surely, only rhetorical anger, bluster, blow. But when she goes back down to the barn that afternoon to milk the cows for the night, leaving me on the bottom step of the back porch, I decide to find my mother and, dressed in my sunbonnet and boots, with Belinda and George and some cold biscuits in a paper sack, I head off down the road.

From two years of farm work I am sturdy, and get perhaps two miles, walking along through the slanting, late afternoon sunlight, while in the east the moon rises in a white sliver. Finally, a pickup truck, driven by the local Baptist minister, stops. He is wearing a dark navy-blue suit; he drives me back to the farm.

(Why didn't Grammy send me back? I was, as she said almost daily, "the worst baggage, the heaviest load," she'd ever carried. I was not, as my mother suggested in letters I should be, "good company for your grammy." I tracked in mud, left doors open and let the house fill with flies and mosquitoes, smeared dirty hands on walls and dresses, broke glasses. If she touched me, I flinched. When her broad, short back was turned, I stuck out my tongue. More than once I told her I hated her, and most of the time I did hate her.)

In wintertime there is less work. Grammy decorates dinner plates with bluebirds, robins, blackbirds, cherry trees. She cuts out and sews clothes from feed sacks, makes tea towels, mends linens, embroiders cross-stitch patterns onto pillowcases. In winter she lets me help her make pies, giving me my own piece of pie dough to roll out, and helping me make cinnamon sugar to sprinkle on them. Grammy makes pie dough with lard for shortening, and with quick strokes, she rolls it out onto a flour-sprinkled wooden breadboard with a wooden rolling pin my uncle bought her that had, she says, "ball bearings" in the handle. For fillings, she uses whatever is in season, and in winter uses the berries, peaches, and pie cherries she had canned. She simply heaps up the fresh fruit or the canned into the pie shell, adds sprinklings of flour, sugar, and pieces of butter. If she decides the fruit does not have much taste, she adds cinnamon and nutmeg. If she has time (or company coming), she makes lattice crusts which she "gussies up" with cutouts (sketched out on the rolled-out crust with the tip of a knife) of cherries, apples, profiles of birds, or what she calls a "heaven top," a round sun with a smiling face, stars of varying size, perhaps a few clouds and a crescent man-in-the-moon. These are stuck to the crust with beaten egg white. She never fails to smile when she does this, and for a few moments, even a whole day, I think I will soon love her.

• • •

Perhaps by keeping me, Grammy was trying, in part, to make amends to my mother for leaving *her* behind in Albuquerque, and then, two years later, giving her to my uncle—twenty-four then—to rear, which he did.

Certainly Grammy was "land-greedy," according to my uncle, who loved her dearly—and who had borrowed heavily in the mid-thirties to buy his mother that farm.

My mother sent her fifty dollars each month for caring for me. In the forties, fifty dollars was not an insubstantial sum.

Grammy was lonesome, and frightened her son would be killed in Japan, and that she would be left entirely alone in the world (she said this, often), for she never much cared for my mother. (Many years later, when my mother would sometimes drink a martini, she would weep, recalling that Grammy cursed her just minutes before she died.)

Two weeks after my runaway attempt, Hiroshima and Nagasaki were bombed. When the Japanese surrendered, Stell was visiting. That night she and Grammy twirled wildly in their bare feet, ignoring the chiggers that bit their ankles and naked arms. They invited me to dance, but I was too shy, and hung back at the edge of the lawn. In September my mother came for me.

LOCAL COLOR

14

LOCAL
COLOR

A Mexican band—bass, two acoustic guitars, accordion—drives up and down Foothill Boulevard in a rusted white van. They stop at each family-style Mexican restaurant in East Oakland, drag in the instruments, and go from table to table singing and playing.

An elderly man summons them to his table, hands the leader ten dollars, and requests a series of what are called *corres*, political "news" songs. A couple, obviously courting, stands up next to their table and dances a few turns. The accordionist taps out the beat with his cowboy boots and smiles, his handlebar mustache arching.

In nearby Richmond at Little Ricky's, a black working-class bar with live music, Maurice McKinnes and his band play Sam Cooke tunes with Cooke stylings, but with a Hendrix guitar underneath. McKinnes, a tall, scrawny, angular guy in his forties or early fifties, has one lung, and his old lady has booted him out. So he has no place "to kick."

A sporting-life type sidled in from the back, wearing a bright green pin-striped suit, a wide-collar green shirt open at the neck, green shoes, green socks, and a neck of gold ornaments. When he blues-shuffled past the bandstand, McKinnes let his cigarette droop and his eyebrow rise and let go a covey of chords he had choked up high on the guitar neck. He shook his head and laughed to himself. The old guys at the bar shook their heads too, as the dude slid past and greeted a white guy in a three-piece J.C. Penney's suit and California male-menopause Kenny Rogers beard and coiffure. The white guy slipped him a twenty and they retired to the john, from which the white reappeared looking sparkly-eyed and took up dancing again with the black women he was with. Next to him a great-big sweet old man in a worn-out leather coat and cap slow danced. He held the cap decorously over his partner's bottom. He smelled good—Brut and hair pomade.

The blues are going strong in the area. Keesee's Your Place is on Telegraph Avenue just over the Berkeley line. Its patrons, mostly black, treat it like a good neighbor's backyard. They stroll over from the long bar and lean elbows on a rail running alongside the stage and dance floor, calling to each other by name and chatting familiarly. Ivey's is on the edge of Oakland's Jack London Square. Its new showroom is all chrome and carpet; its mirrors reflect sharply barbered black men in dark pinstripes, silk ties heavy on foulard, and shoes polished up to old mahogany, along with women in severe, flattering suits or bright silky dresses with nipped-in waists, shaded stockings, and leather shoes. Men shake hands briskly, women kiss. Between sets you can hear ice rattle in glasses.

Black people were among the earliest residents of West Oakland. During the century's initial decades a steady migration came from Louisiana, Arkansas, Oklahoma, and

Texas. Many settlers came to take railroad jobs; West Oakland grew up around what is now the Amtrak depot at 16th and Wood. During World War II the population increased rapidly when men and women moved to Oakland to work in local shipyards. Older, larger homes were made into apartments to house the influx.

The neighborhood attracted entertainers to its clubs. In 1933 when Prohibition ended, Harold "Slim" Jenkins opened a nightclub at 1748 7th Street. Big names in black popular music—the Ink Spots, Earl "Fatha" Hines, Louis Jordan, Dinah Washington, and Ivory Joe Hunter, who put 7th Street on the musical map by recording "7th Street Boogie"—entertained Jenkins's racially mixed audiences, although in many clubs a white line, painted across the floor, divided white from black sections.

In 1950 Esther Mabry, who had been a cook in Jenkins's restaurant and banquet room, left to go out on her own. She opened Esther's Breakfast Club. In 1961 she added Esther's Cocktail Lounge, and after Slim Jenkins's building was sold in 1972 and Jenkins moved his club to Jack London Square, Mabry opened Esther's Orbit Room.

During the height of West Oakland's blues boom, a young impresario named Bob Geddins began to record the neighborhood's gospel groups and bluesmen, and the recording sessions fostered the local clubs like Three Sisters, Rhumboogie, Slim Jenkins's, Manhattan, and Esther's Orbit Room. Geddins recorded blues artists in the back of his radio repair shop at 711 7th Street, then at Down Town Recording Company on San Pablo Avenue, and eventually in his own studio at 539 11th Street.

•   •   •

Born in 1950, Maxine Howard grew up with seven brothers and sisters in a two-story row house a few blocks from Geddins's recording studios and the 7th Street clubs. The Orbit Room was one of the first clubs where Maxine performed when she was still a teenager.

"I got my fire from my mother," Howard said. "She's a

determined woman. She was the strength. And church! I mean, *every* Sunday! Church! We were raised in Reverend Carl Anderson's St. John Missionary Baptist Church, at Eighteenth and Market. An' we used to spend most of Sunday there."

Never trained to be a singer, she never learned to read music. "It grew up with me," she said. "When I was eight or nine my father had his own group, the Southern Travelers. They would sing at the Seventh Street Star of Bethel Church and the Seventh Street Mt. Calvary Church. But they practiced in the living room, all of them singing a cappella. They didn't have all that madness with guitars and drums.

"Our family had a church group, too, the Howard Family Singers. The music *seeped* into us. We all started singing as kids by trying to imitate what we heard. Then I got into choir. I was the lead singer in Local Number Three, which is still going strong. We'd meet every first Sunday from three in the afternoon until eight or nine at night."

St. Matthews was one of the first churches where she sang. Also the Three Sisters, an after-hours club that used to be called Allen's. "It was all drag queens back when I was seventeen or eighteen an' I used to go in there. And the way I dressed, they used to think I was a man in drag, too.

"The *women* who have inspired me: Billie Holiday,"—Howard starts ticking names off on her fingers—"Tina Turner, Koko Taylor . . . Ma Rainey . . . Bernice Reagon and Sweet Honey in the Rock, Joni Mitchell, Holly Near, Esther Philips . . ."

When Maxine Howard was in her early twenties, her brother Woodrowe Howard, Jr., put together a band called the Third Express, with Ronnie Stewart, another guitarist; Kenny Winters on keyboards; and a drummer named Duck. Woodrowe Jr. wrote a lot of original songs and they played local clubs for two or three years. After that, she worked with several male bands.

"I did that for too many years. You're the woman out front shakin' your ass and lookin' good, and they're gettin' the credit. I saw that being a chick singer, up there shooby-dooin', didn't say shit. And I didn't find it flattering. I decided if someone's gonna pimp me, it would be me, Maxine, doin' the pimpin'."

In 1977 Howard put together her first band, Combination Max. She hired Stewart and Winters from the Third Express days. "For the first time I was taking charge of my material. And it felt good. I was growing into a woman-oriented singer. I was changing lyrics around to a woman's advantage, not just singing despair." Three years later, Howard formed the Down Home Blues Band with Stewart as her guitar player, Winters on the keyboard, George Mustafa on percussion, and Richard Lewis on bass.

The blues, Howard says, "*is* male-dominated" in both its performers and its musical content. It hasn't always been that way. Harlem vaudeville singer Mamie Smith's recording of "Crazy Blues" ignited the blues explosion of the 1920s. OKeh, Paramount, and Columbia records recorded the black women known as "classic blues singers," women who performed in vaudeville and minstrel shows—Sippie Wallace, Victoria Spivey, Sara Martin, Ma Rainey, Alberta Hunter, Ida Cox, Bessie Smith, Clara Smith. The classic blues singers worked with jazz pianists. But after the twenties, there were never again so many women singing the blues. Why?

"Maybe it's not for a lady to do—just cold down-hearted blues. Maybe women prefer disco clubs—to be cutie pies, to be ladies. Perhaps it's conditioning. It's fashionable to sing jazz, scat, lady songs. But singing blues is so *out there*. And this is still the age of bein' cute. But it's changing. Listen, last year I put together a night of Bay Area Women in the Blues. It was Margie Turner, Shirley Jackson, Lady Rose, Ella Pennywell, Sarah Levingston, Dottie Ivory, and an a cappella women's group, the Stoval Sisters, and myself. We sang all night, yeah. It was gorgeous."

Up close the fine chiseling of Maxine's features show: high cheekbones, dimples at the corner of her mouth when she smiles, strong chin. She is also tall—five-eight, she says, with heels adding another two or three inches.

"You hear performers talk about 'knockin' 'em dead,' 'killin' 'em,' " she says. "Well that's bullshit. I don't like it. I *in-spire* my audience." She stretched the last syllable with a gospel singer's melisma and a southern softening. "I don't knock 'em dead, and I don't want to. I want them to feel more alive. I want to sing music that's so good an audience can eat it like food."

Maxine Howard emptied five or six packets of sugar into the coffee and stirred in cream until the cup was pale.

"When you sing the blues, who you are shows through. You can't fake it, your nature shows. In blues . . . what can you *feel?* That's what counts. I have the willpower *and* the strength. You can have the will but still be weak. I'm no cutie pie. I'm a strong woman and I'm *proud* of it.

"I'm *proud,*" she intones, almost magisterially, "to live in the *black* community. I don't live *in the ghetto.* People say 'ghetto' to us to keep us discontented, so we'll say"—her voice rises to a squeal—"I live in the ghet-to. I'm not happy.' " Back to her own low-pitched tone: "But I'm happy here. I don't feel stifled. There's a lot of work to be done, right here. I'm not goin' *any*where.

"I got pregnant when I was sixteen. When Mahalia was born," she chuckled, "I wanted to name her Maxine Jr. but somebody talked me out of that! I named her after Mahalia Jackson.

"After I had Mahalia, I left home. I got a studio apartment. It wasn't much. Mahalia slept in the kitchen and I slept on the couch. But it was mine. I was determined when she was born I was not going to be dependent on Mama.

"Of course the greatest education for a woman is to deal with a man. Mahalia watched me dealing with men, and she learned.

"I never used drugs, alcohol, or smoked. And I didn't allow it in my house. I never wanted her to be like me. But I did want to inspire her to be independent. And she is. She's *gorgeous.*"

Asked if she's ever been married, Howard looks quizzical.

"Be serious. Can a cow whistle? I've *never* been married . . . and I *never* will be. I'm wild," she says, looking stern, "but I'm not loose. Wild women," she says, echoing the Ida Cox song, "don' get the blues." And she laughs.

• • •

Eli's Mile High Club at night is dark. And the lighting, in the corners and at the back of the stage where it isn't dark, is yellow. Maxine Howard has a four-piece band behind her, including guitarist Ronnie Stewart and keyboard player Kenny Winters, both of whom have been playing with Maxine for thirteen years. Stewart starts the evening off with "Got My Mojo' Workin," and then takes the group into a funky, sassy version of "Crosscut Saw." Slowly the dance floor fills.

By the time Howard takes her place in front of the band, the room smells of perfume brought out by the sweat that is running down dancers' faces. The screaming conversations stop.

"I'm Maxine Howard . . ." she tells the crowd as she steps out in front of the two black-suited guitarists and the drummer, ". . . an' this is my Down Home Blues Band."

Her pink Lurex trousers glitter. Light gleams off her bare brown shoulders.

". . . an' I'm a woman!" Her clear, strong voice vibrates with passion. "I'm a ball of fire!"

Her tall, slender frame is willowy and glittering pink. Her tongue is pink and her open mouth; her brown high-cheeked face, distorted. She racks up power and builds the song, shakes out the da-ta da-ta rolling of the drums. She tattoos the floor, the three-inch heels on her boots doubling time, then doubling time again.

"Sing it, Maxine," a basso voice shouts.

"I'm a ball of *fire,*" she wails. "I can make love to a crocodile . . ."

The voice is throaty, fierce, choked. The eyes, closed. All that shows is the black line of lash. She's walking the words high off the ground, she can't let go. She has one more inflection left on her long breath and a hush falls on the dark room. She has the only light. Maxine Howard starts out slowly—swaying, riding up her last line of high notes, squeezing it out easy, easy . . . and then she's on top, pouring forth round full sound. "I'm a rush of wind," she sings, and the storm of her voice breaks wide open.

"Yeah, yeah, tell it, sister," someone shouts.

"I'm a woman . . ." Smiling, beaming, triumphant, she raises up her arms. "Is anybody out there *glad* to be alive?"

The crowd, slapping hands, exults with her. She makes a chorus of the crowd.

Howard, always high-energy, is boiling. Her dark brown eyes lock with the quieted audience and she shouts out again Koko Taylor's refrain of Bo Diddley's "I'm a Man": "*I'm a woman.* I'm gonna go down yonder behind the sun . . . Do somethin' for ya' you ain't *never* seen done . . . Hold back lightnin' with the palm of my *hand* . . . Shake hands with the devil and make him *craaawl* in the sand . . ."

She hisses: "I can cut stone . . . with a pin!" Her tall frame pulses. A vibrato quivers her brown throat.

Howard lays down the mike and moves out among the small, crowded tables. Her voice stays full and round, driving with fervor out on top of the band. She urges them higher—higher with their own jubilation—rolling her bare shoulders, shaking herself out, knocking out rhythms and fast blues shuffles.

Even after Mahalia was born, Howard never stopped singing. She was *always* singing. She babysat for a woman who had lots of records. She remembers how she played and replayed "Summertime" and sang along. "The neighbors," she said, "would knock and ask if they could come in and listen. Then a woman I was babysitting for sneaked me into the Showcase Lounge in Oakland, and we signed me up for the talent show. I sang 'Today I Sing the Blues' and I won."

After that Maxine Howard took her first paying job as a singer. She sang lead for an all-male group at the Showcase, Marvin Holmes and the Uptights. "We did songs like 'It Takes a Lot of Good Lovin' to Make a Satisfied Heart' and Etta James' 'Tell Mama'. Top Forty with soul was what Marvin did."

She sang for a year at the Showcase before moving to Esther's Orbit Room. It was during the last decade, as Howard looked for music that had substance, songs that lent themselves to her fiery, independent nature, that she—as she puts it—"grew into the blues."

Blue. A curious word. Some believe it is derived from *blow* and *bruise*—that green-yellow, blurring into *blue,* left on skin by a blow. Whatever the etymology, blues is a rhythmically complex music with an emotional range from celebratory to funereal, from jump to dirge. It is rooted in African music and has its ritual power. It is incantatory, numinous, god-invoking. It healed, soothed, ensured prosperity. By the 1700s *blue* had also come to mean downcast and depressed. Yet *blue* has always had a light as well as a dark meaning. On the light side are the unclouded skies we associate with perfect pleasure. Blue, the color of constancy: true blue.

In the black community, the middle class has tended to shun the blues as vulgar. Urban dwellers regard it as unsophisticated, while people from the country find that blues songs remind them of what they moved their lives to get away from. This may be part of the reason blues performers attract proportionately larger white than black audiences. For too many blacks, it's a link to bad memories.

Blues tells about troubles between women and men, about sexuality's raw power: "It ain't the meat it's the motion/that makes your mama wanna rock . . ." It speaks of the ways desire can bring on betrayal, hard times, long cold lonesome nights, and even colder hungover dawns. The flatted notes cry out with anguish, the lyrics are of mortality's darkness: unrewarding work, sickness, homelessness, servitude, the end of love. Wandering, strange rooms, train whistles. Home, too—of coming home to hambone and collards and beans, or Louisiana's red beans and rice and hot pepper. Its flatted thirds, fifths, and sevenths urge on the raunch of naked longing. Its rhythms demand movement. The blues sing bleak hopelessness like no other music.

In its earliest days, when a lone man sat down with his guitar and sang, what he sang tended to be inward and introverted. Though the blues ensemble grew to include harmonica, gut bucket, washboard, and then store-bought percussion, electrified equipment, and more than one voice, the inward habit stayed.

In the spare, unadorned verses, stripped of adjectives and dependent on sonority for end rhymes, in the bleak halftones and the minor keys, out of B.B. King's vibrato and Robert Johnson's bottleneck, in the grunts, moans, splats, wails, and writhing gut cries of singers, comes the "song" of what it is to be alive here on this earth, rich or poor, but mostly poor.

Like the church music from which it came, these lyrics also talk about hope. Blues is the music of real life, life without the guarantees—music that hopes beyond hope. It urges hearers to keep on keeping on, even against waves of relentless despair.

• • •

The West Oakland BART station and the main Oakland post office now take up entire square blocks of Howard's first neighborhood. The BART trains shoot across the elevated tracks above still-green patches through which, Howard says, she used to walk when she went to school or down to Jefferson Park.

Howard's parents, Vivian and Woodrowe, came to California in the the thirties from Texas. Mr. Howard worked at Todd Shipyards. "He was a good father. We never had much. We never, for instance, had a car. We bused it everywhere, or we walked. But he made sure we always ate. And my mother, she grew a big garden."

Esther's Orbit Room is quiet at noon on Saturdays. Up at the bar a few men hunched over their beers look up at the football games on the color TV. In the back, Faye Wells and

Elnora Stewart, who worked at Esther's during the days Howard sang there, have been cooking, and Howard is hungry.

Esther Mabry remembers Maxine was very thin. "You used to be a whole lot skinnier, didn't you, Maxine?" Elnora Stewart teases, even while Maxine is trying to decide what she wants for lunch.

Maxine pulls up the back of her sweater out of the bronze leather trousers she is wearing and shows off the rose-printed pajama top under the sweater, saying: "It's cold out. I'm wearin' my pj's!

"We've got to get out of the sterotyping of the blues as sad, sad, sad," she says. "All that crying over the mike. All that pain. We seem to elaborate on black people's pain, and on women's pain. The sad blues feeds that between black men and women . . . feeds the condition in which they're *both* victims.

"Take Billie Holiday—her pain has been exploited. I'm sure that woman had some happy days. But what we use from her life is her pain. If I was in the audience, I wouldn't want to be *bothered* with all that mis'ry. I come out to a club to forget the madness.

"A woman singing the blues *has* to switch this sad bullshit around. You have to take the initiative to turn a song around and make it your own, to make the music positive for women an' to give men a new outlook.

"The average blues song is a 'somebody done somebody wrong' song. And it's usually the woman's done some man wrong. He's workin' hard all day, and she's out spendin' his money. I want to say somethin' positive that brings men and women together instead of repeating all that old bullshit that keeps us apart. I could sing 'I had me a man that was no damn good.' But what for? Do we elaborate on our pain? Or do we try to take ourselves out of it? Check it out!"

On the jukebox, over the blare of the football game on TV, Gladys Knight and the Pips sing 'You're Number One (In My Book).' Howard says, "It's important for a woman performer to emphasize *joy.*" She opens her mouth wide. *"Joy* . . . because there are a lot of *miserable* women out there. Women have been hurt."

What if you hit the big time? I ask.

"I don't have much money," she says, laughing, "but I'm rich as hell." She is in control of her music, in charge of her life. And "No," she says, "I won't quit at the hospital." She has a day job in a San Leandro convalescent home, where she's worked for eight years. "Those ladies, they need someone around who understands what it is to be old. It takes a lot to get old, you know. They need somebody who won't call them 'Dearie' or 'Jean,' but who calls them, with respect, 'Mrs. Smith,' 'Mrs. Jones.' I don't want *ever* to lose my connection there."

MAKE BELIEVE

15

MAKE
BELIEVE

I still had pigtails when I first met Carlisle Floyd; this was in the mid-fifties. He was, I believe, the first adult I was allowed to call by first name. Dark-haired, brown-eyed, a cleft cut in his chin, he couldn't have been much older than twenty-five. I was twelve. He taught piano at Florida State University in Tallahassee, where my mother, a soprano, took a Ph.D., and, later, taught. They became friends. Carlisle had, by then, written several one-act operas.

I preferred the "race" records I could tune in between sunrise and sunset broadcast by Tallahassee's black radio station, songs like "Lawdy Miss Clawdy," the Clovers' "One Mint Julep," Joe Turner's "Honey Hush." While I sat in the music building auditorium as Beethoven's "Appassionata" was played and thought of what I would do when I finally got old enough to leave home, I was, nonetheless, quite interested that Carlisle was a man who "made art." This person with whom I would share a platter of smoked pork chops and a serving bowl of buttered Uncle Ben's rice, this everyday sort who sometimes went to the movies three times a week and who stirred pineapple juice into his iced tea—would, after eating dinner in our kitchen, go home to the card table beneath a gooseneck lamp in his living room and "create."

He was an artist, like my grandmother. My grandmother painted plates and gourds. Executed in a Grandma Moses style (but without the charm), they were just plain ugly. I knew that, even in sixth grade. But the pleasure that suffused her jowly face when she got a bluebird to settle on its leafy bough was an *extasis* that even I—who did not like her—could not deny.

Carlisle was working on his first full-length opera, *Susannah,* whose libretto was based on the apocryphal book, *Susanna and the Elders.* Over three years the project moved from idea to libretto to music. In costumes my mother had sewed at night on her old Singer, with orchestral parts I copied for Carlisle at a dollar a page, *Susannah* had its first performance in Tallahassee.

By the time I met Carlisle Floyd, several phrases were riveted into my mind: "You can't make a silk purse out of a sow's ear"; *Creatio ex nihilo*; "Thoughts are things." The first came from my maternal grandmother, who saved rags to braid rag rugs and who painted robins and bluebirds onto the gourds raised on vines in her garden and the white china plates she got with trading stamps. The second I found in the old blue *Webster's,* in the back where foreign phrases were listed. The third was my mother's moral standby.

"Ars longa, vita brevis," which was cut into stone above the doors to the music building where Carlisle and my mother taught, and where I went for piano and violin lessons.

Carlisle was from South Carolina, born a few years before the Great Crash, son of a Methodist minister. He had struggled financially to get through undergraduate and graduate school. He was the first adult I had observed close up who took reading seriously and who approved of my voracious appetite for books. He lent me Modern Library editions of Dos Passos, Faulkner, Sinclair Lewis, Eudora Welty, Robert Penn Warren, Steinbeck. What he was doing, all those evenings at the card table, I understood as making "thoughts into things." I began to understand that almost everyone wants, and even needs, to make something pretty. The Latin cut above the music-building door meant that art endured on earth, where *things* counted, whereas a petty human life just shucked its mortal skin and then was buried and forgotten.

In 1965 Carlisle Floyd began thinking about writing an opera based on John Steinbeck's *Of Mice and Men.*

• • •

Steinbeck is as California as you get. His paternal grandfather came West from Massachusetts in the 1870s. His father—John Ernst Steinbeck—grew up in Hollister. In 1894, having variously worked as an accountant, feed-store proprietor, and treasurer of Monterey County, he settled, with his schoolteacher wife, in Salinas. In 1900 the Steinbecks bought a gingerbread Victorian house in Salinas in which, two years later, John Jr. was born. A shy, jug-eared boy, he grew up reading his mother's books and hoping to be a writer.

Steinbeck attended Stanford erratically during the twenties, his classwork disrupted by his writing, which he did in his father's discarded double-entry ledgers. When not at Stanford, he bucked hay, helped build the first road below Big Sur, and clerked in an Oakland men's clothing store.

The days that preceded his writing *Of Mice and Men* were Steinbeck's happiest, although he was poor. His manuscripts were making the rounds of New York publishing houses, and Steinbeck wrote to a friend, "the pen feels good to my hand. Comfortable and comforting. What an extension of self is this pen."

Steinbeck applied part of the proceeds from *Tortilla Flat* toward the purchase of a two-acre lot fifty miles north of Monterey, near the then quiet little town of Los Gatos. While the house was built, Steinbeck stayed in a wood-shingled Pacific Grove cottage, at work on a "new little novel" about two itinerant ranch hands. He called it *Something That Happened.* In the beginning, Steinbeck apparently had a theater piece in mind. Although accounts vary, it is probable that the idea of writing a play had its genesis in a visit Steinbeck received from John O'Hara after the latter had been hired by a Broadway producer to turn Steinbeck's *In Dubious Battle* into a play. In February 1935, Steinbeck wrote his agents, "I'm doing a play now. I don't know what will come of it."

By April 1936, *Something That Happened* had come along, but at the end of May, he wrote his agents: "Minor tragedy stalled. My setter pup, left alone one night, made confetti of about half of my manuscript book. Two months work to do over again. It sets me back. There was no other draft. I was pretty mad, but the poor little fellow may have been acting critically. I didn't want to ruin a good dog for a manuscript I'm not so sure is good at all. He only got an ordinary spanking."

Steinbeck began again. This time his story was a book and it had a new title, *Of Mice and Men,* from the Robert Burns poem about best-laid plans. By early summer a draft was finished. His agent and his publisher liked it.

Steinbeck did not expect *Of Mice and Men* to do well. But early in 1937, just after his thirty-fifth birthday, the Book-of-the-Month Club selected his work. A month after publication it had sold one hundred thousand bookstore copies. As a play, *Of Mice and Men* went to Broadway the following year, and the year after it became a movie starring Burgess Meredith as George and Lon Chaney as Lennie.

Carlisle Floyd's first version of the libretto was too close to the novel and play. For the second version, he took the advice of a friend, who told him to write his own *Of Mice and*

Men, "to simply assume that I had pretty well digested both book and play." What remained, said Floyd, were only the story's absolute essentials, "with much less dramatic padding and more room for lyrical expression." As an example, Floyd cited a duet in Act 3 between Lennie and Curley's wife. (As Act 3 opens Lennie has accidentally killed his puppy; he is trying to hide its body in the hayloft when Curley's wife enters, carrying suitcases. She is leaving Curley.) Neither aware the other is speaking, Curley's wife and Lennie each muse on the future—Lennie will have his rabbits; she will go to Hollywood. Floyd "found this so operatic that it begs for music."

By the time *Of Mice and Men* opened in Seattle in 1970, the dramatic line had been pared down to the bone. As the curtain came down that January night in Seattle, audible sobs emerged from the audience. But moments later the mood was exultant, as if we had all miraculously survived some act of God, and people rose from their seats applauding, crying out for the principals, the director, the conductor, then "Author, Author!" I was in my late twenties and had babies at home and was taking a course in Shakespeare's tragicomedies by correspondence.

Twenty years later the opera sounded in my life again. My daughters were grown, I was in California. *Of Mice and Men* was being mounted by the Berkeley Opera Company.

• • •

Richard Goodman is a civil-engineering professor at Cal. He is also the artistic director of the Berkeley Opera Company. In Goodman's office, opera posters decorate the walls. An IBM screen glimmers with equations. The Berkeley Opera Company was born out of Goodman's longing for a company that would perform less frequently heard words by European composers, and opera written originally in English: Ralph Vaughan Williams's *Sir John in Love,* Benjamin Britten's *Albert Herring,* Samuel Barber's *Vanessa.* Opportunities for vocal soloists are few. "It's very competitive, especially for women, and particularly for sopranos. As many as sixty will typically show up for auditions for roles, even though the company can offer principals no more than five or six hundred dollars—a pittance for the several hundred hours of work required.

"I never wanted to be a producer, and I still don't," says Goodman. "I'd happily turn this over to somebody else, but it seems always to be that there is somebody who wants a thing to happen and makes it happen and if it *weren't* for that person it *wouldn't* be happening.

"The public doesn't realize when they go to the symphony, and say, 'Isn't that terrific?' that these events are always carried on the back of a few people who put them together, who give the money to make them happen. It is always going to be that way in our society."

In 1979 Goodman produced and financed performance of a one-act opera, Sir William Walton's *The Bear*. Although the opera was vocally demanding, it was, Goodman said, "funny as can be, not avant garde, and very comforting to the audience. People came. Not very many, but the ones who *did* come were very enthusiastic." Goodman was hooked.

Richard Goodman has final say on which operas will be produced. "But there are forces at work I have to satisfy. The conductor has to agree it can be sung and learned by the orchestra. It has to be something we can build sets for. The costuming has to be reasonable." Goodman wanted, for instance, to do Moore's *Ballad of Baby Doe,* but "the designer ruled it out because one scene is a ball at the presidential palace. We couldn't afford the ball!"

Marin, Novato, Petaluma, Oakland, San Jose—all boast opera companies. In most instances professional singers are cast in leading roles and amateurs or part-time professionals take lesser roles. Professionals design sets and costumes. Volunteers build and sew. Typically, the orchestras use nonprofessional, nonunion instrumentalists. One flutist in the Berkeley Opera orchestra sells real estate. The oboist is an X-ray technician, the bassoonist a school administrator. The timpanist is a student. There are teachers, a biologist, a veterinarian, and retired persons.

Opera is not cheap. The production budget for *Of Mice and Men:* $3,500 for sets, lights, costumes, and props; $3,065 in salary for the conductor, singers, and director; $1,800 for publicity and printing; and $3,000 for the twenty-five orchestra members.

About half the annual total total budget comes from ticket sales. The company has almost never had grant support. The financial needs not met by ticket sales are provided by Richard Goodman.

He hopes the audience will grow, yet he does not want to see the company expand significantly. "All men kill the things they love," he said, quoting Oscar Wilde. "I always think of that. You get involved in something you love. You build it bigger and bigger. Before you know it, it eats you alive and you don't love it anymore. Or you can't do it anymore."

For the past four years the company has worked out of the auditorium of Martin Luther King, Jr., Junior High School. When the company first moved in, the auditorium was in disrepair, the stage lighting did not work, curtains were torn, seats slashed and, because of budget cuts, the school could not afford to keep the hall cleaned. "Before one performance when I should have been resting," Goodman said, "instead, I was running a vacuum steamer to get filth out of the carpets. My wife was scraping chewing gum off seats and scrubbing off graffiti."

A "sitzpro" is the initial rehearsal for orchestra and singers together. The orchestra had held its own and the singers had worked extensively with a pianist. This was their first joint runthrough.

Shouldering tubas and bass viols, toting a canvas-jacketed cello on a hip, orchestra members hurried up stagedoor stairs into the dark auditorium.

By 7:20 P.M. the instrumentalists were tightening and loosening pegs, screwing in mouthpieces. A violinist rubbed her bow across a rosin block and white dust rose. Arpeggios and vagrant melodies from sonatas and *concerti* stirred through what would be the orchestra pit.

Conductor Khuner's father has played in several orchestras conducted by his son. The elder Khuner turned to the man next him and lamented that he hadn't gotten to his garden that afternoon.

Half-painted flats filled the rear of the stage. Trees rose across one flat. The log interior of the bunkhouse had been blocked out on another. Midstage stood a table and five chairs.

Lola Watson, a luminescent coloratura, wore a red sweater, black leather pants, and high heels. She was well cast. With a rounded body and strongly delineated features, her presence, off and on stage, seemed unselfconsciously sensual.

Paul Tavernier is the pleasant-faced man playing Candy. He graduated from Yale with a master's degree in performance, then moved to the Bay Area in 1977, ready, he said, "to make it as a musician." The first three years he washed dishes at a hospital. Finding that "a nowhere place to be," he trained to become a respiratory care practitioner, and works with critically ill patients. Tavernier has played Capulet in the Marin Opera's production of *Romeo et Juliette* and sung in Berkeley Opera's *Luisa Miller.* He sings for pleasure and as escape from the "real horrors of the world." "If I miss a note," he said, "nobody is going to die of it." *Of Mice and Men* was coming closer to what he did at the hospital than had other operas. "Usually the musical part of my life is a little lighter. This piece is wrenching. It tears at you. Even though those things aren't really happening, you have to act as if they are. You have to believe they are. It is not fun."

Jonathan Khuner lives in Oakland, where he conducts the all-volunteer Prometheus Symphony. He is a conductor, pianist, violinist, and mathematician. He is also a prompter and coach at the San Francisco Opera. Khuner is the son of a violinist now retired from the San Francisco Symphony and San Francisco Opera orchestra. Khuner was on his way to a career as a mathematician when he discovered "how it would feel to be a mathematician for a living." He turned back to music. As Khuner walked to the lectern, a young woman nearby suggested to her companion, "Jonathan has the perfect hair for a conductor."

Prefatory statements followed about the music: "melodious, appealing, legible and powerful, reminiscent here and there of Copland, Puccini, the Russians. . . ." Khuner, score open before him on the lectern, explained that Floyd, like Wagner, uses leitmotivs to mark specific characters, dramatic elements, events. At Khuner's nod, a woman seated at a grand piano played a portentous melody. The piano was so out of tune the passage sounded perilously close to accompaniments hammered out on old uprights for silent movies. "This melody," said a wincing Khuner, "will recur each time trouble is in the offing."

Setting the scene for the first of several examples of the leitmotiv principle, Khuner says that the opera's opening scenes follow the novel's early pages. George and Lennie are introduced as they are once again, escaping from the police, two itinerant ranch hands who dream of owning a small house and farm of their own.

Stories like *Of Mice and Men* tell themselves. They have what Joan Didion calls "narrative inevitability." You don't explain this story, you have to tell it—"once upon a time." *A few miles south of Soledad, the Salinas river drops in close to the hillside bank and runs deep and green.*

At Khuner's direction, Goodman and Becker sang from act 1, scene 1. "Did you have to touch that girl's dress?" Goodman's George chastised Becker's Lennie. "Couldn't you just have looked?"

"I just wanted to feel it," Lennie sang in reply.

Right foot forward, arms out, palms turned upward, his head thrown back in a grand operatic stance; Goodman played to the taller Becker. I found my mind wandering into questions of art.

The score demanded skill and concentration. Carlisle Floyd's instrumentation had been cut in half for this smaller production, the tendency of the orchestra to drown the voices had to be contended with, and the hall, without an orchestra pit to allow voices to soar out over the instrumentalists, was awful for the singers. As Khuner worked through the score, problems surfaced. For one, the instruments were overpowering Goodman's vibratory bass. I couldn't understand one word the ranch hands sang.

The scene shifted to the bunkhouse where Curley, the ranch owner, complains to Candy, the bunkhouse man, that his new hired hands are late for the first day's work. Leaning over the podium, Khuner talked with the orchestra: "It's more important you play rhythms than the exact right note." So this is how art ends up, I thought. Goodman came out into the auditorium where he whispered with his voice teacher, who was taking notes on the rehearsal.

On stage, Curley and Candy rose from their chairs. The orchestra members' lips showed they were counting. *"Standin' me up! Makin' me wait! Shiftless, lyin' scum!"* Curley's darkened tenor seeped menace. In "real life," Ross Halper works as a stage actor and in TV commercials. Holding his score, and wearing jeans, sneakers, and a white T-shirt, Halper had begun to turn himself into the arrogant, hot-tempered Curley.

Lola Watson stood to face him, jumping an octave. The violins took off beneath her iridescent coloratura, and the elder Khuner vigorously plucked pizzicati. "Lousy, no-good bums," sang Halper, answered by a chord plucked across the harp. Curley gives her no attention, she will get it where she can: the duet ends in a violent quarrel, with Curley ordering his wife to stay out of the bunkhouse. She takes her leave, singing, "To think I could have been in movies, and I had to marry *you!*" Watson sat down, her eyes still blazing.

It is not easy to match the commonly held image of "opera"—opulent, harmonically thick tales of star-crossed lovers punctuated by now-we-stop-everything-and-sing-arias—with this story of Steinbeck's, set in a time and place where cold biscuits were spread with lard and California's agriculturists, already buying up small farms and creating conglomerates, fought pitched battles with grizzled homeless men in patched boots, a landless proletariat living out of jalopies.

The flats were only half painted; the singers left books and conversations to rise and sing, shifting in and out of roles. Khuner called frequent stops and starts.

Even with all that it was becoming easy to forget this was only make-believe.

The company moved slowly on through the score—past the shot that kills Candy's dog, past Lennie's lyric plea for a pup and George's ominous reference to the shooting. Khuner finally called for a rest.

Since Wednesday night there had been two rehearsals, but this was the first dress rehearsal. Khuner addressed the orchestra. "Listen to the intonation, so that it sounds pleasing to the audience, and not just like some strange modern music." A police siren opens the overture. "I come in, I bow, then I will let that siren go just two, three, seconds before the curtain rises." The house lights go off.

Goodman wore a dark shirt, an old slouch hat, and dark trousers of the kind that used to be called "work pants." The stage was lit to suggest a campsite at night. Becker's Lennie wore overalls. His face, huge and albino-white, rose spectrally out of the staged gloom. As much as Khuner had hushed the orchestra, Goodman's voice remained lost in the light wielding of strings and winds.

Act 1, scene 2, the bunkhouse. Eric Landiman, the set designer, had created a Joseph Cornell box of girlie pictures, razors, blanket rolls, a checkerboard. Candy's old dog, chained to a table leg, thumped her tail. When Curley's wife, Lola Watson, made her entrance, she stepped on the dog. The cast broke down giggling and the orchestra ground down like a rough engine dying.

Order finally restored, the proceedings stuttered on. The dog was led out to be shot. Candy lay on his bunk, back to the audience. Lennie sat on the top bunk, aping emptiness while George, on the lower bunk, mimed hypersociability. The ranch-hand chorus did so much busy stage business they could have been miming the Mad Hatter's tea party. The small space had become almost comically crowded.

As the rehearsal progressed, the ensemble got tighter. Although their voices were still largely buried by bunks and flats, Halper, Watson, and Becker were cutting a clearer swath for their characters.

I asked Goodman what got him into this. He laughed. "Being Jewish." Goodman grew up in Forest Hills, New York. His mother was a housewife and pianist, his father a dentist who loved music. His mother dragged him to the opera and ballet. Young Richard showed little interest in opera. He preferred the ballet. By fourth grade, Goodman quit elementary school.

"Every morning I left the house at eight, got on the bus, then on the subway right at rush hour, got off, took another bus, then walked a couple blocks and ended up at Spielter's School of Modern Piano Technique, where about twenty kids studied." Many of his peers at Spielter's went on to Manhattan's High School of Music and Art. But Goodman entered his neighborhood high school. He left high school two years early, and at seventeen was a junior at Cornell, majoring in geology.

After taking a master's degree in civil engineering, Goodman worked several years in industry, then came to California for a Ph.D.

He became involved in an opera workshop in which he was assigned the role of Sharpless in a scene from *Madama Butterfly*. "Sharpless has almost nothing to do in this scene. Occasionally he asks, 'Can I read you this letter?' and then the soprano sings again. It was such an *experience* for me to try to do this, to make it seem as if I were trying to read a letter. I was frightened to death. It was the biggest challenge I'd ever faced, to sing the words nicely, to keep the correct pitch, to remember the words, come in on time, *and,* all the while, to pretend you weren't doing any of it, but rather thinking the thoughts of the character. That seemed impossible. I didn't know how *anyone* could do that."

American operas have always had trouble finding an audience and are rarely recorded. Goodman first heard *Of Mice and Men* in an archival recording of its performance by the Des Moines Opera. *Of Mice and Men* is not Carlisle Floyd's best-known work. That is his earlier opera, *Susannah,* which had its New York premiere in 1957 and has been performed across America and in Europe. Floyd, who teaches at the University of Houston, is also the composer of *Wuthering Heights* and *Willie Stark.*

• • •

The Goodmans' daughter, Lily, collected tickets at the auditorium's doors on Sunday afternoon. Wearing black dresses and tuxedos, the orchestra was tuning. A red velvet curtain covered the stage. Just after two o'clock the concertmistress stood and drew an A from her violin. The orchestra matched her note. Khuner walked briskly to the podium, bowed, ran his hand through his dark curls. The siren sounded.

As a result of the fury raised by *The Grapes of Wrath,* Steinbeck, at forty, left California. Some critics suggest that once Steinbeck left home, he never found another subject. Near his life's end after the Nobel Prize had been awarded him in 1962, he came back—only to find that California as he remembered it was long gone.

I had until now avoided seeing the opera's last scene. I had asked Goodman if he identified with George. At first, he said, he hadn't. "Being a professor is so different from being a man who lifts bales of hay all day long." But once on stage, yes, he had begun to identify. "It's easy to identify with a person who loves another person. But it's tough to act it."

When the curtain came down, the woman in front of me wept. Across the aisle, a man took out a large white handkerchief and wiped his eyes. Then, row after row, in waves, the audience began to applaud. The cast turned to us and bowed. Khuner swept his hand across the ensemble and the orchestra rose. Enthusiastic cheers greeted Goodman. I thought of the bluebird on my grandmama's china plate.

On the street, two teenagers walked ahead of me through lemony sunshine. One was short, plump, freckled, and flushed, the second tall and muscular, a basketball cradled against his belly. His friend carried the radio, tuned to a station playing Whitney Houston's lush "You Give Me Good Lovin'." "What do you like about that?" I asked the smaller boy.

"Aw, it gets *down.*"

Copyedited by Margaret Wolf.
Designed by Frank Lamacchia.
Production by H. Dean Ragland,
Cobb/Dunlop Publishers Services, Inc.
Set in Garamond by Kachina Typesetting, Inc.
Printed by the Maple-Vail Company on acid-free paper.